HOW TO CREATE AN UNSTOPPABLE

MARKETING & SALES MACHINE

An Introduction To Fusion Marketing

CHRISTOPHER RYAN

Fusion Marketing Press

ISBN 978-0-9825397-2-9 (paper)

ISBN 978-0-9825397-3-6 (electronic)

Book and cover design by Van-garde Imagery, Inc.

This book is dedicated to my wonderful wife,
Peggy Ryan. Thanks for your support, your friendship
and for being an outstanding life partner.

Contents

Introduction

*"Because its purpose is to create a customer, the
business enterprise has two—and only these two—basic
functions: marketing and innovation."*

-Peter Drucker

Welcome to *How to Create an Unstoppable Marketing and Sales Machine*. I assume you are reading this book because you want to achieve major improvements in your marketing and sales operations. Perhaps you would like to create an unstoppable marketing and sales machine. That is great, because I can show you how to make this happen. There is much more for your reading and learning pleasure as well, including:

- How to synchronize and optimize marketing and sales for maximum effectiveness

- How the new social media techniques can catapult you to success

- How to hire and motivate a team for outstanding performance

- Low-cost marketing and sales techniques that can beat larger competitors

- How to create major marketplace awareness for your company and products

- The best ways to plan, monitor, and report on marketing and sales progress

- How to rescue a failing marketing or sales operation

Although I wrote this book primarily for marketing professionals, it will have a great deal of relevance to the sales manager, business owner, and corporate executive. If you are new to the marketing role, it will help you get to the next level, and if you are a veteran marketer, it will keep you on top of your game. You will also benefit if you have primarily been using traditional marketing techniques but need an update on using the new media.

What I bring to this book and to you, the reader, is a great deal of relevant experience, tested in twenty-five years as both a business-to-business marketing service provider and a senior marketing executive at companies ranging from start-ups to billion dollar enterprises. I also bring a history of rolling up my sleeves and producing outstanding results. This book is not about theory—it is about what I have done and what I continue to do to help companies achieve massive awareness, produce hundreds of thousands of qualified sales leads, and generate hundreds of millions in revenue. Most important, it is about how you *can* and *will* do the same.

As the graphic below illustrates, we all have six resources to use to achieve our objectives: people, budget, programs, content, processes, and technology. You may feel that you lack the right quantity and quality of these resources to win at the marketing and sales game. However, it is not only what you have, but also how you optimize and synchronize your resources that determines your outcomes. That is the essence of Fusion Marketing: bringing the parts together in such a way that they create a greater and more powerful whole—similar to what happens when tiny atoms are brought together (fused) in such a way that they create massive nuclear energy.

**Fusion Marketing – Creating Results
with Synergy and Optimization**

How to Create an Unstoppable Marketing and Sales Machine is organized into seven sections. Part one covers ways to build a strong foundation for success. Part two talks about how to plan and measure the results of your marketing efforts. Part three shows you methods to build your unstoppable marketing and sales machine. Part four teaches you how to align your marketing and sales departments for outstanding results. Part five gives you options for media and related tactics. Part six talks about how to manage and motivate a superior team. Our final section, part seven, shares advanced marketing strategies such as viral marketing, selling on a small budget, and what you need to do to rescue a troubled marketing operation. The intent of the book is to show you how to personally accelerate your marketing and sales results, or to impart knowledge which will give you the ability to manage employees or contractors to accomplish this.

Since I have brought so much thought, effort, and experience to the endeavor, I would like you to invest a few things as well, to ensure that you receive real results for your business. I would like you to bring your curiosity about what makes prospects tick, your open-mindedness to new ideas, your willingness to take a few risks, and the confidence that allows you to make a few mistakes, learn from those mistakes, and constantly improve at marketing and sales.

Although marketing is still under-appreciated in many executive suites, I strongly believe that it is a noble and exceedingly important profession. In fact, in the new interactive and social media era, marketing is often the most important determinant of a company's success. Good marketing (and sales) often beats a superior product, and the sky is the limit if you have both. While sales managers are fond of saying "nothing happens until a salesperson sells something," the fact is that you cannot make a sale until a marketer has first properly done his or her job.

Here's to your future success. Happy reading.

Christopher Ryan
cryan@fusionmarketingpartners.com
www.fusionmarketingpartners.com

Part I

Building a Solid Marketing and Sales Foundation

Chapter 1

How to Thrive in the Changing Marketing Landscape

Characteristics of a High-Powered Fusion Marketer

"The more things change, the more they remain...
insane."

– Michael Fry and T. Lewis

Twenty-five hundred years ago, the Greek philosopher Heraclitus stated, "Nothing endures but change." Therefore, change is certainly not new. What *is* new is the pace of change. Evolving economic systems, globalization, advancing technology, and other factors have created a climate where every aspect of business has been transformed, and sometimes in a very short time period. Likewise, the marketing world has changed a great deal over the past few years. New technologies and tougher economies have combined to force a massive shift not only in the techniques of marketing, but also in the way we think about the subject.

If the above were not enough, consumers are changing in ways unfavorable to traditional marketers. They are becoming smarter, tougher, and less prone to acting like sheep willing to be sheared by the skillful marketer. Today, the buyer does the shearing and the marketer loses his coat.

The fact is, we have long since left the Mass Marketing Era, and are now in the Era of Pinpoint Marketing, where individual decision-makers will be harder to find, their job functions will change more often, and the means of converting them to customers will be different. Your ability to identify qualified individual prospects is a key determinant of marketing success, along with the ability to speak to their unique needs and deliver offers that are timely and compelling.

Education can certainly help you, but a bachelor's degree or an MBA is no longer enough to insulate the marketing manager from obsolescence. Yes, the fundamentals are important, but marketing is becoming an increasingly technical subject, and experts readily acknowledge that the half-life of a college degree in most technical subjects is no more than three to five years. This means that roughly half of what you learned at even the most prestigious university has a useful life shorter than your new car.

The answer to the changing marketing landscape is to adopt the characteristics that will help you not only survive, but also thrive.

Characteristic 1: A Fusion Marketer Stops What is Hurting

"Call on God, but row away from the rocks."
                                                    – Hunter S. Thompson

Most of this book is dedicated to telling you what you should be doing to turbo-charge your marketing and sales performance. Fusion Marketing is a "damn the torpedoes and full speed ahead," don't look back, and take no prisoners style of marketing that is designed to have you focusing on your objectives and leaving your competitors to eat your dust.

But before we get into all the good things you can do, let's talk about what not to do.

In an interesting *MADtv* skit, Bob Newhart plays a psychiatrist whose entire practice is based on telling his patients to stop their dysfunctional thoughts and behaviors. He doesn't analyze them to death, he doesn't look for origins in childhood, he just tells them to "stop it." If you have ever been to counseling, you may have wished that the good doctor would just come out and tell you to stop whatever it was that caused you to be there in the first place. You don't have to be a Bob Newhart fan to enjoy the humor and message (and you can easily find it by doing a search for "Bob Newhart Stop It" at youtube.com).

The "Stop It" skit is very funny, but it also makes a useful point. The first step on the road to recovery is to stop doing that which hurts you or which does not make a positive contribution to your well-being. We know this to be true regarding our personal habits, but how do we apply this to marketing—how do we intelligently *stop it*? We do this by taking a sober assessment of our campaigns, strategies, programs, expenses, etc., and immediately stop:

- Anything that does not have the support of senior management.

- Lead generation programs that are not followed up by the sales team.

- Campaigns that do not reinforce your core message.

- Expenses that do not contribute to the overall objective.

- Unnecessary and/or time wasting reporting and analysis.

- Working with people who are unreliable and/or unproductive.

- Anything that you are doing as a manager that is impeding your staff's ability to get their jobs done quickly and efficiently.

The list of potential things to stop can be much larger (how about unnecessary meetings?). Remember that everything you spend time on has an opportunity cost – something more productive you could be doing. In this sense, you are competing against yourself: your smart and efficient inner marketer is competing against the knucklehead and sloppy marketer. You just have to let the good guy win and tell the knucklehead to go away.

Likewise, everything you spend money on has to be evaluated against all the other ways you could spend the same amount of money. If you determine that the expense is not worth it but you don't really have anything else worthwhile to spend the money on, you can try something really unusual—give the money back to the company. Your CFO will love you and you will feel like a first-class corporate citizen.

It may be tempting to tell your coworkers about all the things they should stop doing. After all, it is always easier to be a critic than a doer. But whatever your job function, start there and lead by example. Positive change begets positive change, especially if you are the first change agent.

Characteristic 2: A Fusion Marketer Plays to Win

> *"Winning is a habit. Unfortunately, so is losing."*
>
> – *Vincent Lombardi*

I would like you to agree with me about something: You are playing to win. Not just your company, not just your department, but you, the person reading this book. I will talk about what it means to win and how to set your specific objectives, but the point is, it is a lot more fun and a lot more satisfying if your mindset is to beat your competitors and win the game.

As I write this, the recession is still raging, companies are closing, layoffs are occurring, and people are scared. But the fact is, even in a bad economy, there will be winners and there will be losers. Your place on the leader board will be determined not only by luck, or what you do, or what industry you happen to be in, but also by your attitude and expectations. It is tough enough to succeed in good times—you are always fighting for business that your competition wants as much as you do.

While confidence is important in any endeavor, it is especially true in marketing and sales. You must believe that you have the right product or service; you must believe that it offers real benefits; and you must believe that you are promoting it to the right individuals. If you have such confidence and play to win, you will have no problem following Dennis Waitley's words of wisdom, "Success is almost totally dependent upon drive and persistence. The extra energy required to make another effort or try another approach is the secret of winning."

The economic trend may be poor. And yes, it is tougher to generate leads and revenue. You may have to work harder to produce the same result. But this is the time when leaders are made. You must think of yourself as not just a victim of economic circumstances but rather as a man or woman who determines your fate by your own thoughts and actions. Whether your job is to generate leads, write copy, design promotions, qualify leads, or sell, a positive attitude will set you apart and give you a better chance of success than joining the doom and gloom crowd.

Recessions do end and the economic pendulum swings from good to bad and back again to good. As you read this we (hopefully) may be back to positive times. But what I said about playing to win is just as important in good times as in bad. And not only is it important, playing to win is a lot more fun.

However, keep in mind that there is a difference between playing to win and playing not-to-lose. If you play not-to-lose it is almost guaranteed that you will not win. Even if you have the best attitude and take the right actions, you cannot always control the outcome. As they say, stuff happens to thwart even the best intentions. You will have to make many tough choices to get into the winner's circle, and many more to stay there. However, it is much easier if your goal is to thrive and not just to survive. In any sport or business competition, if all else is equal, I will always pick the person who has the best attitude, — the one who is determined to beat his competitors and take the prize.

Characteristic 3: A Fusion Marketer Practices Laser Focus

> *"The shortest way to do many things is to do only one thing at a time."*
>
> *–Sydney Smiles*

In an article published in *Early to Rise*, noted business strategist Rich Schefren stated that when people tell you something can't be done, they really mean people can't do it without taking themselves out of their comfort zone. To develop laser-like focus Schefren advises the "back pressed up against the wall" mindset. To do this, you pick a goal you have been struggling with—and then you tell yourself that if you don't achieve that goal, the person you love the most in this world is literally going to die. If that were the case, your back would be pressed against the wall. You would suddenly get a lot more focused on achieving that goal because you would *have to* do it.

Thinking about the potential death of a loved one is a tough way to make the point, but the fact is, Schefren is correct. We do have a much better chance of achieving what we focus on, especially if we get rid of the many distractions that deter us from our path.

The British philosopher Isaiah Berlin divided leaders into foxes and hedgehogs. He suggested that hedgehogs are individuals who relate everything to a single, all-embracing principle (big time focusers), while foxes are those who see a multitude of things without necessarily relating them to one universal system (not so focused). In the business world, the fox may see more of the big picture, but lacks the clarity of vision and single-mindedness of the hedgehog. In the political arena, Ronald Reagan was a hedgehog and Bill Clinton a fox.

Does this mean that foxes can't succeed in marketing and sales? Absolutely not, and in fact, foxes that know how to operate like hedgehogs can be extremely successful. If you are a fox, you need to fight the tendency to go to the next thing when you get bored or when the marketplace doesn't go your way. And if you are a fox manager, you need some hedgehogs around you to help you stay the course.

I am a fox by nature and I can easily see the big picture and the way multiple parts work together. I can also juggle many different strategies and projects, and focusing doesn't come naturally to me, at least for long periods of time. But I have learned to separate my personal inclinations from what works in business and I always have people on my team who can stay focused on the primary objective.

I have seen a lack of focus ruin two companies I was involved with and conversely, I've designed a laser-focused marketing strategy to help make several others highly successful. One of the two losing companies had great potential but literally changed its strategy on a quarterly basis in an attempt to placate hungry investors. One quarter the company was going to be a low-cost software vendor, the next a services company, then an OEM supplier, then a high-priced customized solutions firm. The company could have been successful with any of these models had they just picked one and stuck with it. The lesson is that persistence and patience are necessary ingredients in the focus stew. While an occasional company benefits from constantly shifting its focus, many more fail due to a tendency to give up too quickly on a workable model—had they just stayed the course, they could have been successful.

So what is my message? Simply this: Spend all the time necessary to pick your go-to-market strategy. But once you do so, do not easily give up on your strategy. Focus and persistence will win the day more often than brilliance. Stay the course, my friends, stay the course.

Characteristic 4: A Fusion Marketer Flouts Conventional Wisdom

> *"By three methods we may learn wisdom: First, by reflection, which is noblest; second, by imitation, which is easiest; and third, by experience, which is the bitterest."*
> *–Confucius*

If you want to stand out from the crowd and achieve Fusion Marketing success for your organization, it is vitally important that you start to recognize some of the common fallacies that pervade the marketing profession. Following are some often-repeated marketing and sales misconceptions:

Conventional Wisdom: Marketing is always expensive.

Truth: Expensive is not always necessary or even better. Many marketers overemphasize the upfront cost of an advertising program, such as the cost to reach a certain number of people, rather than the more important gauges that tell you if your program is profitable, such as cost-per-sale or cost-per-dollar-of-revenue. The techniques in this book explain how you can spend less on marketing and produce greater results.

Conventional Wisdom: Consumers are no longer loyal to products or organizations.

Truth: Consumers are not inherently disloyal, and they display this trait only to the degree that they are conditioned to be disloyal. Companies that place major emphasis on attracting new customers and minor emphasis on retaining existing customers should not be surprised when the latter start doing business with the competition. Properly implemented relationship marketing techniques can forge strong bonds of loyalty between you and your customers. In fact, relationship building is not only critical to the marketing function—it is one of the major attributes of a well-run organization.

Conventional Wisdom: A great product will ensure your success.

Truth: You need to aggressively promote even the best products and services. A recent University of Michigan study determined that more businesses fail due to inadequate marketing than for any other reason. The fact is that most of our products are not as superior to the competition as we would like to believe. It is an axiom in the technology industry that some of the largest and most successful companies have mediocre to average products, and some of the outstanding products have been consigned to the dustbin of history, *because of poor marketing*. Our task as marketers is to make our products stand out from the many choices available to consumers, because while product quality is often a subjective measure, marketing efforts produce either positive results or lousy results.

Conventional Wisdom: Knowledge about your products or services is the most important key to success.

Truth: While it is vital to understand the details of your products or services, particularly regarding how they benefit customers, this is not the most important factor. Knowledge of the potential customer is even more important. If you know who your customers are, and know their needs, desires, and buying influences, you will find if far easier to construct your message in such a way as to motivate them to action.

Conventional Wisdom: Marketing is just a corporate expense.

Truth: Marketing is an investment, not an expense. The fact is, if you follow the methods in this book, you will be able to quantify the return on investment (ROI) of your marketing programs. Just as important, especially when budget cuts are on the table, you will be able to show how reducing the investment in marketing will directly lead to a reduction in revenue. I have been in these discussions, and the ability to link marketing to revenue has kept my budgets intact, and has sometimes led to increased funding.

Conventional Wisdom: Following the rules and statistics of marketing will guarantee success.

Truth: As noted above, things change very quickly in today's marketplace, so you must be careful to ensure the rules you follow are not based on yesterday's environment. Moreover, if there is one thing more dangerous than a rule, it is a statistic. Remember that someone with his head in an oven and his feet in a bucket of ice water would have an average temperature in the comfortable range, but don't try to tell him so. Relying solely on rules and statistics is guaranteed to make your marketing boring, and boring does not sell.

Conventional Wisdom: Creativity is the most important factor in marketing.

Truth: Creativity may be fun, and it may be interesting, but I have seen countless so-called *creative* promotions that totally failed to meet their objectives. In fact, some of these campaigns even win industry awards. Such campaigns can be worthless at best and terribly costly at worst. To be effective, creativity must be married with the right offer, presented to the right audience at the right time, using the right media.

Characteristic 5: A Fusion Marketer Does Whatever it Takes

"It's not enough that we do our best; sometimes we have to do what's required."

–Winston Churchill

What exactly did Churchill mean by "doing what's required"? This is not a trick question—he meant that we must do *whatever it takes*. Not what feels good, or easy, or what comes naturally to us, but rather that which is necessary to accomplish the mission. Do not confuse these things, because the level of commitment is often what separates the winners from the has-beens. There are some people who have enough natural talent to achieve a level of success without putting out the effort, but they are the exception, not the norm.

In marketing and sales, doing whatever it takes means that you do the tough upfront work to make sure you have a compelling value proposition. You research your competitors and know their strengths and weaknesses. You look at every possible sales and distribution model and conduct tests to determine which is best for your products and/or services. You gain intimate knowledge of your target audience, including their demographics, pains, desires, and requirements. You find the best and most appropriate media to reach these people. You hire and train salespeople who can close business. You continually refine your processes to achieve the greatest amount of revenue at the lowest acquisition cost.

Doing whatever it takes also means that you make the tough choices. You are willing to admit when you are in the wrong market. You change course when necessary, but you stay the course when others want to throw in the towel. Despite the emotional and financial investment you have in your people, you make the hard personnel choice when it is good for the company. You fire the salesperson you like when he or she does not perform, and you keep the person that you don't personally care for, because he or she is a real asset to the company.

My only caveat to doing whatever it takes is that what you do must *always* be done with integrity and decency. Shortcuts that involve lying, cheating, or being incongruent about who you are may appear to be effective, but are very often harmful in the long-term.

This willingness to do "whatever it takes" truly separates those who *wish to be* successful from those who *are* successful. If you are facing a competitor who will do whatever it takes to beat you, you are in for a rough go of it. However, if you (and your organization) are focused and willing to do whatever it takes, as an individual and as a company, you will be a blessing to those who depend on you and a curse to your competition.

To summarize, here are five characteristics of a high-powered Fusion Marketer:

1. Stops what is hurting

2. Plays to win

3. Practices laser focus

4. Flouts conventional wisdom

5. Does whatever it takes

Success Tip: Adopt the five characteristics of a high-powered Fusion Marketer.

Chapter 2

Avoid the Seven Deadly Sins
of Marketing and Sales

"It is said that if you know your enemies and know
yourself, you will not be imperiled in a hundred battles."
– Sun Tzu, The Art of War

Since the title of this chapter is "Avoid the Seven Deadly Sins of Marketing and Sales," I thought you might like a reminder of the original seven deadly sins: lust, gluttony, greed, sloth, wrath, envy, and pride. While the marketing equivalents are not as serious, they are areas that, if not addressed, can lead you to marketing and sales disaster.

Deadly Sin 1: Lack of Self-Awareness. When I refer to self-awareness, I am talking about not only understanding who you are as a marketing or sales professional, but also where you shine (or don't) as a company. We could call this environmental awareness, because the work environment is where you spend your time every day, and is influenced not only by the people in the environment (coworkers, etc.), but also by outside forces like customers, partners, and market conditions.

Sun Tzu would have made a heckuva marketer because he understood that knowledge is the best weapon. But I think it is sometimes harder to truly know one's own nature than it is to know others'. This is because of the natural tendency to see yourself not as you are, but as you wish to be. Psychologists refer to this as the *perceived self vs. actual self*. To be truly self-aware you must be willing to take a frank look at your weaknesses and strengths.

For most of us, our weaknesses can be found opposite our strengths. If you are studious and contemplative, some may see you as standoffish. If you are aggressive and persistent, some may view you as obnoxious or a bully. You get the picture. It is also true that others can be more objective about you than you can be about yourself, because they are more emotionally detached. This is why it is said that people care more about their own hangnails than about 100,000 starving children in Africa. Not because we don't all care about hungry children, but because we experience an emotional detachment.

On the company side, self-awareness means acknowledging when your competitors are better at certain things than you are, and vice versa. To really understand your organizational strengths and weaknesses, read the chapter on completing a SWOT analysis. If you do this in a spirit of openness and truth seeking, I guarantee it will be time well spent.

Deadly Sin 2: Perfectionism. There are certain areas of life where perfectionism is highly valued—brain surgery and symphonic music are good examples. However, in marketing and sales, the need to be perfect can be counterproductive. You might be questioning my sanity right about now—after all, what is wrong with striving to create perfection in our marketing and sales efforts? Well, there is actually a lot wrong with this trait. The struggle for perfection can freeze you into inaction. Here are some reasons why perfectionism can be a liability instead of an asset:

- The extra effort required to get something from ninety percent quality to perfection is exhausting—perhaps as much as was required to create the original ninety percent.

- Perfection is very subjective. One person's perfection is another's mediocrity. Sometimes you can work on something until your fingers bleed and your brain hurts, and there will still be people who don't like it (especially other perfectionists). As Herbert Prochnow noted, "A great many people mistake opinions for thought."

- Perfection is elusive. No matter how hard you work, there is always more you can do.

- The struggle for perfection can creative havoc with your staff, especially if they perceive that what they produce is seldom good enough. People who work for a boss with perfectionist tendencies tend to resent the boss and lose a sense of ownership in the outcome.

Early in my career, I worked for a boss who was highly critical of everything I or anyone else wrote. He could never let go of striving for perfect messages, perfect copy, etc. Once he actually criticized his own writing, forgetting that he had authored a particular piece himself. It was a miserable experience for me, and I wanted to shout on more than one occasion, "Take a chill pill! We're not trying to write Shakespeare or paint the Sistine Chapel."

Note that I am not encouraging mediocrity in any fashion. You need to be very good at what you do. However, *good* and *perfect* are two very different things. You need to realize that consistency and quantity of output are important characteristics of productive marketing, and a needless (and fruitless) search for perfection can be a detriment to your success. When you are tempted to pursue perfectionism, remember the words of Voltaire, "The perfect is the enemy of the good."

Deadly Sin 3: Living in the Past. This is one of those areas where past success can lead to future failure. The world of sales and marketing (and almost everything else) has changed dramatically. While some of the core strategies and techniques mentioned in my three earlier books are still valid, others are not even mentioned here because seven years have passed since my last book was published. I would guess that some of what worked for you just two to three years ago may now be obsolete, let alone what you did ten or twenty years ago.

While Andy Grove's book *Only the Paranoid Survive* was written for a general business audience, the title applies equally well to marketing managers. A good marketer is a paranoid marketer—always wondering what new techniques others are using to gain competitive advantage. It's a big world out there, and by the time you have figured out how to do your job, others are taking it to the next level.

One of the best ways to prevent living in the past is to be a watchful consumer. Keep an eye out for how companies are marketing and selling to you and emulate the best practices. Borrowing from good ideas is perfectly legitimate as long as you do not copy anyone's text, designs, and so on.

Deadly Sin 4: Failure to Quantify. When John Adams said that "facts are stubborn things," he meant that people find it convenient to ignore or hide the facts when it serves their purposes to do so. However, in marketing and sales, data is your friend, not something to be shunned. It used to be that the big advertising agencies avoided hard metrics like the plague. Their efforts were about brand awareness and the only thing they measured was how many creative awards they won last year.

In tougher economic times, with competition from every corner of the globe as well as cyberspace, most organizations cannot afford to measure results in soft terms—rather, they need hard data that tells them how many people are seeing each promotion, how many are responding, and how prospects are being moved through each stage of the end-to-end process until they become customers. There is a great deal of useful information about how to measure marketing and sales programs in this book. Please read and practice these recommendations.

Deadly Sin 5: Failure to Test. This marketing sin is related to the "failure to quantify." Marketers who do not test are marketers who don't get the best results. Whether you call it resting on your laurels or staying with the status quo, inertia is your enemy. Programs that work today will tend to deteriorate if you fail to refine them, and the best way to know what needs refinement is to test. Every element of marketing campaigns can be tested, including the target audience, offers, benefits, messaging, media, copy, and graphics.

I recommend that you make testing a formal part of your marketing strategy and budget accordingly, devoting ninety to ninety-five percent of your finances to campaigns that have proven successful (control campaigns), and the other five to ten percent on new programs, new offers, new audiences, etc. Keep in mind that you should not have the same expectation for success with the test budget items as you do for the rest of your campaigns. This is where you experiment, take chances, and roll the dice, in an attempt to beat the control campaigns. It's a fun part of a marketer's job, and it feels great when your test campaign becomes the new *control*.

Deadly Sin 6: Inaction. "When in doubt, attack" was one of Napoleon's maxims for military success, and it is equally true for marketers. There is never a perfect time to enter a market, launch a campaign, or execute a quick hit strategy. Sometimes you won't have all the facts, sometimes you won't know how a target audience will respond, sometimes you won't have the luxury of waiting for all the research to come in, neatly tied up in a bow, with no doubt as to the outcome. However, this lack of certainty should not freeze you into inaction.

Good marketers are aggressive marketers. Just as any athlete has his or her playing field (arena, stadium, etc.), you have your own playing field. That playing field is wherever you can give prospects real opportunities to know you, to interact with you, to enter the sales cycle, and to become customers. And if you are in a fast-paced market, it is sometimes necessary to forget *ready-aim-fire* and instead practice *ready-fire-aim*. You learn by doing, not just by studying, pondering, and analyzing.

Part of my call to action is to urge you to get out from behind your desk and out of the office and go where prospects and customers are. I mean this for marketing people as much as sales people. No matter how smart you think you are, most of the good stuff happens out there, where people are pondering whether to purchase what you have to offer. That is where the knowledge is and that is where the revenue is. You must meet people where they live and work to understand how to sell them better. Go to the trade show. Take a customer to lunch. Go do the presentation. You may find out that what got everybody excited back at headquarters did not resonate when you are behind the podium or trying to explain it on the show floor.

Speaking of headquarters, if you are now a senior marketing or sales manager or aspire to be such, you must make a decision as to whether you are going to be a headquarters general or a field general. Simply put, the field general is willing to go out and make the presentation, meet the prospect, and help to make the sale, while the headquarters general runs the battle from the office. I recommend that you choose the field general route. It is no secret that beloved military commanders like Caesar, Joan of Arc, Napoleon, Washington, and Patton could be found fighting side-by-side with their troops. So whatever type of troops you have (marketing, sales, or other), show them that you are a leader who likes to be where the action is.

Deadly Sin 7: Focusing on What Doesn't Matter. As a marketing or sales manager, you have two primary resources at your command: time and money. I am not sure where I see more waste. Certainly, there is a great deal of money spent on programs and activities that have little chance of success. However, there is also a great deal of time spent on the irrelevant and the counterproductive. You and your staff have a limited amount of time and no doubt, a large number of tasks before you. Every minute you spend on a nonproductive activity hurts you in two ways, first because you wasted time on something that is not helpful, and second because that activity prevented you from spending time on something that is helpful.

Here are some things that do not matter, unless you can show them to have a direct correlation to revenue:

- How many direct reports you have

- How much your staff likes you

- How cool your ads look

- How big your trade show booth is

- How fast your budget grows

- What you did last year (or last quarter in fast-paced industries)

- Time spent in endless and nonproductive meetings

So what exactly matters?

- More leads going to the sales force

- Hiring good people or outside contractors to assist you

- Reduction in wasteful spending

- Cross-selling and up-selling customers

- Changing to a process that improves funnel conversion ratios

- Lowering your cost of customer acquisition

- Increasing revenue

Chances are you can identify several additional items to go on each list—both bad time wasters and good time investments. Many managers who are excellent stewards of their company's financial resources are frivolous when it comes to guarding the most precious resource of all—time. If you concentrate your time on just the stuff that is really important to effective marketing and sales, and drop the rest, you will not only benefit the company immensely, but you may even find a little extra time for the truly important things like family and friends. Wouldn't that be great?

Success Tip: Make sure that you are not guilty of any of the seven deadly sins of sales and marketing.

Chapter 3

Ask the Tough Questions

What You Must Know to Be Successful

"Unless you are the lead sled dog, the view never changes."

–Alaskan saying

At the beginning of any strategic marketing and sales review process, I urge my clients to answer some tough questions about their go-to-market strategies. I suggest you do the same because the answers will determine how well equipped your company is to attack your market successfully.

Tough Question 1: What is The Big Idea? Lee Iacocca once said, "When the product is right, you don't have to be a great marketer." While I believe the statement was well-intentioned, it is also wrong. The truth is, even a great product or service has to be marketed properly to succeed. Your BIG IDEA is that competitive point-of-difference, the value-added extra that makes what you offer unique and better than your competitors.

If you are going to create a powerful marketing and sales engine, then you need to have a clear and compelling marketplace position. Positioning is one of the most misunderstood, unappreciated, and neglected parts of the marketing process. David Ogilvy, famous advertising pioneer and founder of Ogilvy & Mather, stated that positioning is the most important decision made in advertising a product or service. He also correctly noted that successful positioning has far more impact on the results of a promotion than how an advertisement was designed and written.

In marketing, the word *position* is defined as "the manner in which an organization and the products or services it provides are perceived by prospects and customers." Every organization, as well as each product or service, has its own unique position, or more accurately, its own series of positions. An organization can occupy different positions among various audience segments. Sometimes, despite attempts to promote consistency through all product lines, individual products can occupy different positions. People can also have their own unique positions. In fact, as I show you elsewhere in this book, you can gain tremendous benefit from properly positioning your key executives, or the owners of your company if you happen to have a small business.

Although positioning can consist of dozens of subtle factors, the three primary elements that define an organization's position are price, quality (or performance), and service. An organization can be known for its low prices or high prices, for its high-quality products or low-quality products, and for superior service or inferior service. Of course, most organizations are positioned somewhere between these extremes in each of the three primary positioning areas. For instance, a company can be positioned as a moderate-priced supplier of medium quality goods, with fair service. These terms are highly subjective, and I hope you think you do a good job in all areas, but remember that it is the perceptions of prospects and customers that count. You may wish that your organization is positioned in a certain way, but you have no vote on how you are actually perceived in the market.

The three positioning elements of price, service, and quality are shown on a *Triangle of Positioning Excellence*. Please note that when I speak of the word *quality* this not only refers to the durability and appeal of the product or service, but also its performance and functionality.

Price

Quality   Service

Triangle of Positioning Excellence

While it would be nice if the marketplace viewed you as being superior in price, service, and quality, it is extremely difficult to achieve perceived excellence in all three areas. It is, however, possible for a company to occupy two of the three points of the triangle. For instance, a company that has a reputation as a low-cost supplier with excellent service would not also be expected to have the highest quality products.

Likewise, given competitive economic realities, a company known for its first-class products and services is unable to sell those products at the lowest cost, because of the additional costs necessary to produce higher quality. Consumers are sophisticated enough to understand that there is a correlation between the price of an item, its quality, and the service that can be expected from the supplier. So when you brag about having the best quality and service at the lowest cost, realize that you are not fooling any but the most gullible consumers. Wal-Mart is not Macy's, and the corner IT shop is not IBM.

Remember that each element of the positioning triangle is always evaluated in relation to the other two elements. For instance, price is always evaluated by the consumer on the basis of how costly the product or service is, given the performance of that product related to similar products. Likewise, price is factored by the anticipated level of service expected after the sale. Thus, a high-priced product can only support its price so long as the customer perceives good value in quality and service. You simply expect different treatment at Mercedes and Chevrolet dealerships.

One of the problems with positioning is that it can be highly fluid. Not only is it subject to the changing whims of the prospect's perceptions of your company's and product's strengths and weaknesses, it is also dependent on the perceived strengths and weaknesses of all known competitors. You can lose your positioning status, as compared with a competitor, strictly on the basis of that competitor's actions. Of course, this can work for you as well as against you. For instance, a rival whose quality standards slip will make your products look better by comparison.

It bears repeating that in marketing, perception is often more important than reality because the marketplace often operates on current perceptions, not facts. This can be a blessing or a curse, depending on how adept you and your competitors are at manipulating consumer perceptions. Of course, the most effective positioning does not rely on manipulation, but takes full advantage of your true strengths and the weaknesses of your competitors. This is why one of the core principles of Fusion Marketing is to be *congruent*, making sure all your marketing activities and messages match what the buyer receives at the point of service. To ensure your positioning is congruent, thoroughly explore the following questions:

1. At what is our organization superior?

2. What can our people do better than anyone else?

3. How can we translate our existing strengths into a unique selling proposition?

Cream may always rise to the top, but products and companies must be pushed to the top. And the best way of pushing a product to the top is through the development of a unique market position.

Tough Question 2: Whom Are You Selling To? To be successful at the sales and marketing game, you need to make prospect identification a top priority. It may sound simplistic, but you only need to ask yourself two questions to start identifying your market. First, who are the people or organizations most likely to do business with me (buy my product, use my services, join my organization, etc.)? Second, who are the people who are least likely to do business with me? Then, you focus all of your time and promotional dollars at the former group, and none at the latter group.

Although these questions seem easy, coming up with the answers is not. As you will read later, identifying your target audience can be a tricky proposition. Knowing only the rough parameters of the potential universe is not enough. Chances are you cannot define your prospect base as broadly as "the Fortune 500" or "small companies." You will succeed more as you tightly define the market.

Marketing used to be a mass-market game. Competition was weaker, promotional costs were lower, and companies could make a lot of money running scores of advertisements or sending out tons of direct mail packages. Today, costs are higher and prospects are bombarded with more promotional messages than they can absorb. There are also many online media vying for attention. As a result, response rates to almost all forms of advertising and marketing media have dropped—in some industries they are only one-third to one-half of previous levels.

The solution to this problem is *pinpoint marketing*, which can also be referred to as one-to-one marketing or target marketing. Pinpoint marketing starts with profiling customers and prospects, and includes database-marketing techniques to control the timing and messaging of communications. With pinpoint marketing, you spend more on each prospect communication, but because you have qualified the audience so precisely, you can run promotions that are more cost-effective and targeted toward real needs. The bottom-line benefit is that even in times of declining response, your marketing efforts can beat the trend, and the cost of achieving each new dollar of sales can decrease.

One of the fastest and most effective ways to find your target market is to analyze your current customers. Amazingly, many marketing and sales managers only have a cursory understanding of the companies with whom they do business, let alone the individuals at those companies who make the buying decisions. If you fit in this group, you will have to dig much deeper to get a realistic picture of your true market. You need to find the similarities within your existing customer base, in terms of:

- Industries that are represented

- Size of organizations you serve

- Geographic locations

- Buyer titles

- Buyer demographics (age, gender, education, etc.)

Keep in mind that you are not just looking for quantities of customers, but also for the quality. The Pareto Principle will usually apply: twenty percent of your customers will generate eighty percent of your profits. You may find that you have dozens of potential markets, but you need to rank them in terms of revenue and potential. Your highest priority markets will have characteristics such as:

- Profitable

- Low acquisition cost

- Areas where you have domain expertise

- Your products/services fit without major modification

- Your products/services are differentiated

- Competition is weak

- Decision-makers are identifiable

You also need to consider the leveragability of a market. In his phenomenal book *Inside the Tornado*, Geoffrey Moore talked about the bowling pin strategy, where you develop a whole product strategy for one market niche, and then leverage the lessons you learned and your customer references from that niche to go into an adjacent niche. The headpin is the beachhead market segment and every other segment is derived from this headpin.

I have used the bowling pin strategy many times. For example, at a content management company, we first developed an accounts payable automation solution, then leveraged success in that segment to create and sell applications for managing accounts receivable and expense reporting. For a client in the sales force automation space, we took the application from IT consulting practices to engineering firms and then into other market segments.

Please do not jump to other parts of the marketing and sales process before determining and prioritizing your target market segments. This effort will reward you with future success.

Tough Question 3: What Are Your Objectives? Once you understand what makes you different and unique, and to whom you are selling, it is time to set your marketing and sales objectives. Objectives serve as the justification for every marketing activity and each dollar that you spend. The statement of objectives (which is also part of the marketing plan) serves as your marketing destination. After all, you cannot draw a road map until you know where you are going.

Marketing and sales objectives fall into many different categories, including positioning, vertical marketing, revenue, lead generation, and public relations. Let's briefly explore each of these categories.

A. Positioning Objectives – While not as measurable as other objectives, positioning is still a crucial element. State your goals in terms of: how you want the market to perceive your company; how you wish to shift customers' and prospects' perceptions of your products and services; building customer awareness for a new product; developing major new distribution channels for your products and/or services; your positioning versus that of chief competitors; and your goals for market changes in awareness, reputation, and customer service perception. Establish a mechanism to measure your performance in meeting these objectives. One method is to conduct periodic surveys of your prospects and/or customer base. These surveys can be in the form of Web questionnaires, telephone interviews, or person-to-person contact such as one-on-one interviews or focus groups.

B. Vertical Market Objectives – To set vertical market objectives, review the analysis you completed of your existing customer file, determine if you are satisfied with this distribution, and set specific guidelines for those industries where you want to increase your penetration. You can express vertical market goals in percentages: "Increase our share of the market among financial institutions from twelve percent to fourteen percent." Alternatively, you can express them in monetary terms: "Increase annual sales to financial institutions from $220,000 to $310,000."

C. Revenue Objectives – As a marketing manager, you may not be the individual responsible for setting revenue goals. However, your input should be given weight in determining these numbers, since you are so close to the marketplace. This is even more likely to be true in organizations where the sales and marketing functions are closely related or part of the same department. Even if you outline the revenue goals in the business plan, you should still include them in your marketing plan. Because there is probably no more important objective to the organization than reaching its sales projections, tying these numbers directly to your marketing programs is always a good idea. In addition to presenting the overall revenue numbers, you may want to break them down by product line and/or geographic sales territory.

D. Lead Generation Objectives – If your organization uses a two-step instead of a one-step sales process, you will need to become well-acquainted with the subject of lead generation. In a later chapter, I will introduce the subject of conversion ratios. However, if you are already doing a good job of tracking leads using conversion ratios, you should know how many leads at the front end of the process it takes to achieve a certain amount of sales revenue. Another way of computing lead requirements is to calculate how many leads each salesperson requires to achieve a given sales quota, and to multiply these numbers to establish yearly lead requirements. After setting total yearly lead objectives, do two additional breakdowns. First, allocate your lead-flow requirements into monthly goals. Second, apportion the leads by specific marketing category.

E. Public Relations Objectives – Public relations is considered such a soft marketing art that many organizations never set specific goals for public relations activities. This is a mistake for two reasons. First, mediocre PR practitioners hide behind ambiguity in order to mask poor performance. A specific public relations goal makes the PR practitioner accountable for his or her efforts. Second, solid public relations can strengthen the total marketing mix at very low cost. Public relations objectives can include: positive press messages you intend to receive for product and corporate news; publishing a certain number of articles in leading trade publications under a byline of an official of your organization; placing your executives as speakers at key industry conferences; and improvements in prospect and customer perceptions of your company, products, and/or services.

F. Other Objectives – List objectives that do not fit comfortably into one of the above categories. For example, show how you intend to upgrade the quality of your leads by increasing the conversion percentage of leads to sales. You can also list the systems you intend to develop and implement to establish tighter control over marketing expenditures. This is also where you list the objectives for greater efficiency between the sales and marketing functions.

Success Tip: Have a big idea, set objectives, and carefully prioritize your target market.

Chapter 4

Accelerate Your Success with Pull Marketing

"Luck is what happens when preparation meets opportunity."

–Seneca

For many years, virtually all marketing was of the *push* variety, so called because the object was for you to push your promotions and advertisements in front of the prospect. Your job was to push your message and push your offer until you generated the lead or sale. This was also referred to as *interrupt* advertising because you were usually interrupting whatever the prospect was doing to present your offer (e.g., watching television, listening to the radio, reading a print publication, etc.). While some think of push media in traditional terms, there are relatively new media such as Web banner ads, pop-up ads, and predictive dialing that are definitely in the push camp.

In the push model, the marketer is in charge of the timing, content, and frequency of promotions. Prospects are in charge of whether they read or listen to your promotion, and whether they choose to respond. Many marketers seem to feel that their job is to shove enough promotions in front of enough prospects to make their sales goals. Push marketing has been the predominant methodology since the days of the Old West pitchman.

By contrast, *pull* marketing refers to making yourself visible to prospects when they are looking for what you are selling. Instead of pushing your offer at them, you allow them to pull what they want from you. Push and pull marketing require different mindsets. As a practitioner of Fusion Marketing, you should do everything possible to make it easier for people to buy from you, not only at the time they are ready to sign the purchase order or hand over the credit card, but also when they are at the earliest stages of the information gathering (research) process. A sale lost early is still a lost sale, regardless of whether you ever knew the prospect existed.

The greatest boon to pull marketing has been the Internet. It has made marketing more complex but also infinitely more flexible and useful to the purchaser. The greatest successes in marketing are being achieved by those who use social media and public relations to make themselves visible to potential buyers, along with pay per click (PPC) and search engine optimization (SEO) strategies to make sure that prospects find them when either doing research or when they are in the purchase phase. This is a great way to generate traffic and is extremely cost-effective. Online registration services such as RSS feeds and Web-based newsletter subscriptions are also effective pull marketing methods.

Business-to-business marketers love to talk about their sales cycle, which refers to how long it takes to close a deal, from first contact with the prospect until the order is signed. However, one of the advantages of pull marketing is its ability to shorten the sales cycle, if you give the prospect plenty of chances to either learn about you through social media, or conduct research on your Website. If the prospect takes six months from initial research through purchase, he may spend more than half that time in research that does not involve your time-strapped staff, and you, in fact, have only a three-month sales cycle with that prospect. This type of marketing is better for you and the prospect instead of the constant push for them to buy something too early in the cycle.

The following two graphics illustrate the impact that pull marketing can have on the sales cycle. Graphic one shows a traditional sales cycle where contact with the prospect lasts over a period of four months. Graphic two shows a modern pull marketing model where you create an environment for prospects to educate and self-qualify themselves, and even conduct their own needs assessment, before they begin engaging with your sales team. Prospects benefit because they can learn about what you offer in a pressure-free way. Your sales reps benefit because they are dealing with fewer prospects, who are more likely to purchase, thus maximizing their selling effectiveness.

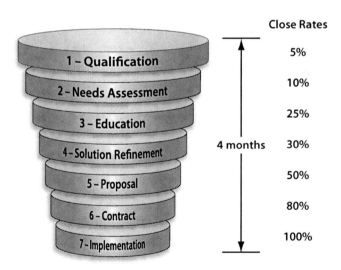

Sales Process – Traditional Model

Sales Process – Today's Model

Most of us will want to use a combination of push and pull marketing strategies. For example, you can aggressively use customized offers to promote your products and services to lists of targeted prospects. However, you can also let the world know about you through awareness-building tools such as public relations and social media. In addition, you can create a content-rich Website that satisfies the hunger of early stage prospects to learn about your offerings in a pressure-free environment. The chapters on Website, social media, and search engine optimization will be particularly important. If you do a good job of pull marketing, you will receive the additional benefit of some terrific push marketing, as your community of believers pushes you to their own social networks.

As you decide how much of your time and financial resources to devote to push vs. pull marketing, keep in mind that the battleground has shifted. As the marketer, you are not really in charge—the prospect holds the high ground. Rather than fight this fact, it is better to accept who has the real control and find the best ways to help people buy in the way they want to buy, instead of the way you want to sell to them.

As a pull marketer, these traits will serve you well:

- Patience: Yes, you should always ask for the order, but accept your prospect's timeframe for purchase.

- Flexibility: Pull marketers require maximum flexibility as they continually search for new ways to inform and please their prospects.

- Curiosity: Develop and maintain a burning desire to learn about your prospects and their characteristics (e.g., demographics) as well as their hopes, desires, wants, and needs.

- Service orientation: The old ways of fooling people or tricking people into buying through superior salesmanship are mostly gone. Those who have a true thirst to serve their customers will succeed.

Success Tip: Get your prospects to come to you by using pull marketing techniques.

Part II

Planning and Measuring for Marketing and Sales Success

Chapter 5

Know the Battlefield

How to Use Research to Understand Your Market, Customers, and Competitors

"You can see a lot by just looking." — *Yogi Berra*

The subject of marketing research has been known to send shivers down the spine of even experienced marketers. They view marketing research as somewhat mysterious and based on complex scientific principles and costly statistical analysis. Yet, the fact is, research doesn't have to be expensive. And you don't necessarily have to pay an outside expert to conduct research for you, although it may be prudent for you to do so. What you must do, regardless of the size or scope of the project, is practice certain time-tested fundamentals. If you fail to follow these fundamentals, the data you generate may be useless, or even worse, counterproductive, because it may be inaccurate or lead you in a direction that is a danger to your business.

A Dozen Good Uses for Marketing Research

Marketing research can be defined as "any activity that involves gathering and/or evaluating information to be used to assist the business decision-making process." Using this definition, marketing research can be used for a great many purposes, including:

1. Identify new markets for products and services – Marketing research can help you find untapped audience segments for your current product and service offerings. These audience segments could be major new prospect groups or narrow market niches.

2. Classify new business and consumer segments by their demographic, geographic, and psychographic characteristics – This is an important purpose of marketing research because you cannot effectively promote to a unique audience segment until you are fully aware of its defining characteristics.

3. Find new uses for an existing product – A product is often shelved because it has supposedly reached the saturation point in its market penetration. Research can help you revive a product and start its life cycle all over again.

4. Test the viability of new products and services – Smart companies want to have an idea of the potential for a new product before spending large sums on development costs. Research can point out modifications that can save a product which would otherwise be a failure. Equally important, research can help you save considerable sums by foregoing products that have no chance of success.

5. Locate decision-makers and influencers – Promotions aimed at the wrong prospect are a great waste of pro-

motional dollars. Locating the right prospect is particularly important in business-to-business marketing since there can be many people involved with the decision-making process.

6. Define the sales cycle – Research can help discover two important questions about the product sales cycle. First, how much time does it take from initial contact through the close of business? Second, what is the internal process that prospects go through when evaluating and purchasing products?

7. Reduce the risk of poor product development and marketing decisions – In a fast-changing, technical world where product life cycles can be as short as eighteen months, business executives cannot afford to make major mistakes in product development or marketing. Research is a valuable tool when it comes to improving the quality of decisions.

8. Test advertising copy, graphics, offer, and message impact before your promotions are seen by the wider audience – As you will read throughout this book, millions of dollars are wasted on marketing initiatives that have no chance of success. Proper pre-testing of promotions will usually increase the chance of success. Post-testing helps refine future advertising so that it gets better over time.

9. Evaluate product or service benefits – It is amazing how often a company is wrong about why consumers purchase its products and services. The only way to be truly sure about the benefits and advantages of a par-

ticular product is to ask the people who know best—existing customers.

10. Determine brand strength and positioning versus the competition – The market is comprised of more than your company and its prospects and customers; it also includes competitors. Your position versus the competition is constantly changing, sometimes in subtle ways, and it is imperative for you to understand these changes. Marketing research can help you do this.

11. Select the best media tools – Poor media selection is fatal to marketing programs. Media planners can use research to help develop media schedules that maximize the cost-effectiveness of every dollar spent on print, broadcast, direct mail, and other marketing vehicles.

12. Track customer satisfaction – Research can be used to get a moving picture of your customers' attitudes about your products, services, pricing, personnel, policies, and so forth. Trends spotted in customer satisfaction can be used to head off serious problems. Many companies are afraid to conduct satisfaction surveys because they are afraid customers will take this as a sign that there are problems. Actually, the reverse is true. Customers like to be asked for their opinions, and consider it a sign that a company truly wants to improve its products and services.

These are just some idea starters and you can probably come up with other uses that are specific to your business. However, the point of research is to help you make decisions that are more likely to produce desired outcomes. But you must always remember that research is a support tool, not an infallible science. Research is meant to guide, not dictate, your decisions.

Success *Tip:* Use research to make better sales and marketing decisions.

Chapter 6

Pinpoint Strengths and Weaknesses with SWOT Analysis

"Nothing focuses the mind better than the constant sight of a competitor who wants to wipe you off the map."

– Wayne Calloway

Socrates was right when he made the observation, "The unexamined life is not worth living," and this applies equally to the individual, the team, the department, and the organization. Everyone, and every company, has one or more blind spots, and your ability to discover these blind spots is critical to the achievement of your marketing and sales goals. However, it is not just weaknesses that you must discover, but also your strengths, opportunities, and threats.

Andy Grove, co-founder of Intel, wrote a famous book titled *Only the Paranoid Survive: How to Exploit the Crisis Points That Challenge Every Company. Forbes* called Grove's book "Probably the best book on business written by a business person since Alfred P. Sloan's *My Years with General Motors*"—quite the compliment (among much other praise). The success of the book is no doubt due to its excellent advice, but also to the way the title and theme of paranoia resonate with entrepreneurs and business people of every stripe. Who doesn't experience paranoia given the tough economic climate, international competition, and rapidly changing technology?

However, it is not enough for you to be paranoid. You need to understand why it is that you should be paranoid. What are the weaknesses in you, your department, your marketing strategy, the company? What are the threats both internal and external that cannot only take you off your game, but also potentially take you out of the game? Frankly, many people do not ask these tough questions because they would prefer not to know the answers. Ignorance can be bliss in the short term, but in the long term, it always catches up to you. Marketing and sales is a tough game, and to play a tough game, you need to be tough. And you can't be tough if you don't root out your weaknesses and find ways to minimize them or overcome them.

Likewise, it is necessary to know the strengths of your opponents (e.g., business competitors) because they will represent threats to you, and the weaknesses of your opponents because they represent opportunities to exploit. After all, marketing is war, and to win at war, you must be acquainted with yourself, your enemy, and the battlefield. As Sun Tzu put it so eloquently in *The Art of War* (highly recommended reading for the Fusion Marketer), "If you know the enemy and know yourself, you need not fear the result of a hundred battles. If you know yourself but not the enemy, for every victory gained you will also suffer a defeat. If you know neither the enemy nor yourself, you will succumb in every battle."

SWOT analysis came from research conducted at Stanford Research Institute between 1960 and 1970, stemming from the need to find out why corporate planning failed. Fortune 500 companies funded the initial research to find a way to overcome poor planning. A SWOT analysis is a subjective assessment of data that is organized by the SWOT format into a logical order that helps understanding, presentation, discussion, and decision-making. The four dimensions are a useful extension of the basic list of pros and cons that many of us use to guide decisions.

According to the creators of the method, SWOT essentially tells you what is good and bad about a business or a particular proposition or category. A SWOT analysis always focuses on four categories:

Strengths – What are we good at; where do we excel; where do we have a unique advantage or significant head start?

Weaknesses – What are we not good at; where are our vulnerabilities; where are we less than adequate; where have we been ineffective in comparison to the competition?

Opportunities – Where can we take advantage of current market trends; where can we exploit our strengths and the competition's weaknesses; what are the possibilities for a big win; what excites us the most?

Threats – Which of the competitors are coming on strong; where are the market trends working against us; what are the gaps that can be exploited by our competitors; what scares us the most?

At the first stage of the process, you are only asking questions, you are not attempting to create action items or set strategic direction. Do not draw conclusions at this point, and do not make any business decisions based on your answers. The point is to get all the relevant input out on the table before you attempt to organize the data and use it for planning purposes. Every SWOT analysis I have participated in has generated far more data than it is possible to work with. After the initial brainstorm and data collection phase, you will need to synthesize the data into the most important and relevant points of data.

Outcomes of SWOT Analysis

As a marketing or sales executive, you will want to perform the SWOT exercise at both the macro level (the entire company or division) and at the micro level (your department). In each case, you perform SWOT analysis to ensure all relevant issues are on the table, to make sure you are gaining consensus from the necessary stakeholders, and to guide actions that have the greatest chance of achieving your objectives. While the outcome is dependent on your particular needs and objectives, in general, you are looking to use each of the SWOT quadrants for issues like:

Strengths – How do we maintain our strengths, build on them, maximize our advantages, and create greater leverage in the marketplace?

Weaknesses – How do we get the team (or company) to recognize its weaknesses, fix what is fixable, mitigate what is not fixable, or utilize outside resources to bring us up to par?

Opportunities – Of the many opportunities we have, how do we prioritize them given our strengths and weaknesses? Where can we get the greatest return on our human and financial investments?

Threats – Which of the threats against us are most likely to derail our business; how do we minimize or counter these threats; what can we do to get out of the line of fire?

An Example of SWOT Analysis

I have used the SWOT exercise for many years, across multiple industries, and for different purposes. Following is an example where I used SWOT to analyze the strengths and weaknesses of a large B2B marketing department. Interestingly, six months later, I ran the same exercise for the same company and found major improvement in almost every aspect of marketing performance. This again proves that it is much easier to improve that which you analyze and measure.

Marketing Programs SWOT Analysis

STRENGTHS
Consistent flow of inquiries/leads
Strong trade show presence
Flexible and responsive to Sales Dept.
Sales development becoming optimized
Reduced conflict between Direct Sales
  and Channel Sales on lead model
Customer and analyst leverage

WEAKNESSES
Reporting, analysis, and communication
Lack of support from field
Lack of search engine optimization
Marketplace awareness is light
Poor strategic alliances
Lack of agreement/focus on key
  initiatives

OPPORTUNITIES
Awareness via Big Splash campaigns
Integrated Web, sales, and market
  systems
Outbound personalization and inbound
  lead scoring and follow-up
Closed-loop system for channel
  management
Viral marketing programs
Focus spending on priority programs
  that drive revenue

THREATS
Unfocused message = market confusion
Sales wanting to change lead model
Market and sales systems not synergized
Vulnerable customer base if we don't get
  the consolidation message right
Competitive giants with large budgets
Growth in number of inquiries without a
  similar growth in number of leads

Success Tip: Perform your SWOT analysis and act on the results.

Chapter 7

Conduct Quick and Effective Marketing Research

"If we knew what it was we were doing, it would not be called research, would it?"

–Albert Einstein

Marketing research is such a specialized subject that we will not go into the mechanics in detail. There are many fine books on the subject. But for most applications, there are eight basic steps involved in planning and conducting a research project. These will be helpful to know whether you decide to do it yourself or hire an outside research firm.

Step one: Establish the study objectives. You must be very clear as to the exact nature of the data to be gathered and the specific purposes for which it will be used. If you fail to establish the objectives, you may fail to ask the right questions. The beginning of the project is also a good time to ask if the benefits of conducting the research are worth the costs.

Step two: Research secondary sources of data. Sometimes the information you are after has been compiled by an indirect third-party source.

Information from these sources is known as secondary research. Sources of secondary research include government agencies (federal, state, and local), industry publications, trade associations, and research firms. You can find a tremendous amount of free or fee-based secondary data via the Internet.

By contrast, you conduct primary research for a specific survey project. For this reason, it tends to be very expensive and time-consuming. While secondary data may not be quite as relevant or timely as primary information, the cost benefits are obvious. Most of the time, you will first want to exhaust your sources of secondary data before conducting primary research. An added benefit of secondary research is that it can help you discover new questions to ask or new information to gather through your primary research techniques.

Step three: Develop the survey methodology. After exhausting secondary sources, determine how you will go about collecting the needed additional data. Sources of direct data include personal interviews, online surveys, focus groups, consumer opinion panels, telephone surveys, and written questionnaires.

Step four: Design your survey sample. Unless you are working with a small, finite universe of potential subjects, you will probably want to restrict your research to a sample of the audience. The key characteristic of a sample is that it accurately reflects the universe. And no, asking your brother-in-law and a few neighbors usually doesn't qualify as a legitimate sample. For a simplified example, if forty percent of the individuals in the potential universe live in states west of the Mississippi, then roughly forty percent of the sample audience should also live in those states. A sample drawing only ten percent of its individuals from western states would be heavily biased toward those who live east of the Mississippi.

Most of the time, it is not the size of the universe that determines the viability of a sample; rather it is the size of the sample itself. If the sample is chosen correctly, only a small percentage of the audience has to be queried to draw inferences about the entire audience. This point is very important, since the same quantity of people can form a sample when the universe is fifteen thousand, or 150 million. For example, during a presidential campaign, only a few hundred people are surveyed at random throughout the nation to predict how each candidate will fare on Election Day. These five to six hundred people can accurately portray how tens of millions of Americans feel about the election on any given day, while the same sample size would be required to predict the outcome of a local school board race.

Step five: Write a questionnaire. Regardless of the techniques used to gather data, you will need some type of questionnaire. Hopefully, your project includes time for exploratory interviews or focus groups which will help to bring up valuable (but previously unexplored) issues, and also to refine the questionnaire itself.

Step six: Collect the data. At the information-gathering stage of the project, your task is to conduct personal interviews, make phone calls, mail out questionnaires, or whatever else is required to collect the needed data. You should also collect the data in as short a time as possible, or the results may be flawed.

Step seven: Compile the data. Once the appropriate amount of data has been collected, it must be sorted and organized. For simple projects this can be a manual process, but more often the information is entered into a computer. Electronic methods of compilation allow for sophisticated data manipulation techniques such as regression analysis and cross-correlation.

Step eight: Analyze and report. After you have collected and compiled all the information, you need to decide which data are important, what the data indicate, and how to present the findings. When you prepare the final survey reports, remember that the individuals reading those reports may not have enough background in marketing research to accurately interpret mountains of data. Whenever possible, keep your reports short and simple.

Primary Research Methods

There are five primary methods used to collect research data. Focus groups and one-on-one interviews are usually used in the early *qualitative* portion of the research project, and electronic surveys, direct mail questionnaires, and telephone surveys are usually used in the later *quantitative* part of the research process. Qualitative research is usually conducted first because it is used to explore broad themes and gather the general perceptions of a small number of subjects.

Once the qualitative phase is complete, detailed questionnaires are prepared and quantitative research is conducted on the entire survey sample. The outcome of quantitative research is usually precise data that you can use to draw specific conclusions about the subject matter of the survey.

Focus Groups

Focus groups usually consist of four to twelve participants who share similar characteristics. For example, you can gather a group of sales reps to explore how they use sales force automation software. You can ask the same group for their opinions on promotional offers, headlines, etc. Information you get from focus groups is usually not sufficient to serve as a basis for business decisions. Rather, you can use the data to help design follow-up survey questionnaires that cover the subject matter in depth.

When you conduct a focus group, be very careful to ask open-ended questions that give no hint of your anticipated or hoped-for answer. Certain people will try to be helpful by answering in the desired manner, regardless of their true feelings. In fact, it is usually a good idea to keep the name of the sponsoring product and company unknown to the participants.

Focus groups are a delicate blend of art and science, so it is usually a good idea to contract with a company that specializes in this type of research. Professional research firms will arrange for all details of the project, including recruiting the participants, facilitating the sessions, and preparing the follow-up reports.

Personal Interviews

One-on-one interviews are a very accurate means of collecting data. In the hands of a trained interviewer, individuals will be very forthcoming with their opinions on almost any subject. The interviewer is there to gauge the level of understanding of the subject and can personally choose subjects to match the desired sample. Just as with focus groups, you should use personal interviews as a qualitative tool, especially in the early stages of a project to help develop questionnaires you can use later.

One problem with personal interviews is that they are an expensive way to collect data. Another obstacle stems from the reluctance of certain people to answer an interviewer's questions. The days of door-to-door opinion polling are almost over since people are afraid to open their doors to strangers.

Web and Email Surveys

There are many advantages to doing your survey electronically, instead of via postal mail or telephone. First, the cost of an email Web-based survey is minuscule compared to other methods (assuming that you have access to an inexpensive list). You can also execute email surveys very quickly. You can design, test, modify, distribute, and compile a Web survey in a week or less. Two tools that I have used for conducting online surveys are SurveyMonkey (www.surveymonkey.com) and Zoomerang (www.zoomerang.com).

The biggest question to ask about whether to do a Web-based survey instead of using the telephone or direct mail is whether you have a decent number of email addresses for potential survey respondents. This is not only a question of quantity, but you must also ensure that your sample is representative of the entire audience—otherwise the survey will be flawed and you will not be able to depend on the data.

Direct Mail Questionnaires

Direct mail survey projects are expensive and time-consuming so you want to make sure the mailed questionnaire is complete, and not lacking in any substantive way. In certain circumstances, such as when the list does not contain telephone numbers, written questionnaires may be the only practical way of collecting the required data. To get the best response rate out of your written survey questionnaire, always adhere to the following guidelines. (Note that many of these principles also apply when you create an electronic survey.)

1. Make sure you interview individuals who have a genuine or perceived interest in the survey's subject matter. This is the primary consideration in the accuracy of the research data.

2. The questionnaire should be easy to read, both from a copy and layout standpoint. To increase legibility, always leave plenty of white space on the page.

3. Keep the questionnaire as short and uncomplicated as possible. It is better to do without a few questions than to go for every shred of data and risk a low response rate.

4. Survey research is supposed to measure how the marketplace feels about a particular subject at a certain point in time. It is a snapshot, not a moving picture. This is why you need to complete the project in a relatively short time frame, and never mix the answers of questionnaires filled out over long periods.

5. Always send a letter with your survey questionnaire. The letter should be personalized if possible, and convince the respondent that she is important and her answers are valuable. Even a short note on the survey form itself is better than going without a letter.

6. Don't forget to tell the respondent why you are conducting the survey and how the findings from the research report will benefit him in his professional and/ or personal life. You must never give the impression that the person's answers will be used to try to sell him something.

7. Give your survey an impressive title. For example, a title such as "Survey of Important Executives in the Information Services Industry" will gain better response than one titled "Computer Industry Survey."

8. Assure the respondent that his participation in the research project will be held in strict confidence. If possible, allow the recipient to answer the questionnaire without revealing his name. Try not to put the

person's name on the survey form itself but, if you must, provide a way for individuals to tear it off before mailing.

9. If you are conducting business research, consider offering each respondent a summary report on the survey's conclusions. Assuming your list contains those who have an interest in the subject matter, your survey will induce many to respond.

10. Put a live stamp on the pre-addressed return envelope. At the least, include a postage-paid business reply envelope. Never ask the recipient to pay the return postage.

11. If you are concerned about the response rate, use a before- and/or after-response booster. One week before you mail the questionnaire, send a postcard notifying the subject that an important survey will be arriving shortly. If the response rate on the first mailing is small, you can also mail a copy of the questionnaire to non-respondents, with a note suggesting they may not have received the original and that you are waiting for their reply. The trick is to be expectant, but never demanding.

12. Consider including a premium with your questionnaire. The right premium can double or even triple response. Successful premiums include coins, dollar bills and advertising specialties such as pens and calendars. Be careful not to imply that you are buying the respondent's time with the premium, but rather are including it "as a token of appreciation."

Telephone Surveys

Telephone surveys have a number of advantages over written questionnaires. For starters, you can get the information much faster. You can develop a program, test, collect the data by phone, compile the data, and prepare follow-up reports in two to three weeks. Telephone surveys also allow for considerable flexibility. For example, perhaps you have conducted fifty phone interviews and several of your subjects raise an unexpected issue. Simply revise the questionnaire and include the new questions on all subsequent calls. This level of flexibility is not possible with written questionnaires.

Many consumers, though, are extremely wary of telephone surveys because they have been subject to *phony* surveys where the real purpose of the call was to sell a product or service, instead of conducting legitimate research. Because of these abuses and the inherent intrusive nature of the medium, a high percentage of individuals will no longer participate in telephone research. Since non-responders tend to fall in certain groups, this means you may not have all segments represented in your sample.

To increase the likelihood of getting your telephone questions answered, keep all questions short and simple. Unless the recipient of the call is deeply involved in the subject matter (or being paid to answer), it is very difficult to keep someone on the phone more than a few minutes. You also want to make sure you represent a cross-section of the universe in your survey. If you are using a master telephone list, do not just tear off a section of the list and start calling. You may be limiting the respondents to a certain geographic area or other segment.

Try to complete each call in a short time period and start out by informing the respondent how long the interview will last. Just as with written questionnaires, it may be better to drop a few questions in the interest of achieving a higher response rate.

Regardless of the survey media or methodology, try not to get too wrapped up in the research project. And do not let it slow you down. As Tom Peters said, you need to "Test fast, fail fast, adjust fast."

Success Tip: Follow these tips on survey methods to ensure the quality of data.

Chapter 8

Write a Winning Marketing Plan

"A good battle plan that you act on today can be better than a perfect one tomorrow."

– General George S. Patton

In today's business environment of *ready, fire, aim,* there is a tendency to react quickly and skip time-consuming steps like market planning. But I urge you not to do this. Although every organization will receive unique benefits, the following are a few reasons why Fusion Marketers spend the time it takes to design and implement a marketing plan. A well-defined marketing plan:

1. Helps you establish marketing priorities. This is very important in the interactive marketing era since there are an increasing number of methods and media that you can use to share your promotional message.

2. Provides you with a timetable for implementing each marketing activity.

3. Gives you specific targets to aim for in the form of marketing objectives.

4. Serves as a barometer for measuring the progress or lack of progress in achieving your objectives.

5. Helps the organization discover the most cost-effective marketing activities for promoting its products and/or services.

6. Gives the marketing team a blueprint for action and specifies the responsibilities of each person involved in its implementation. Since bureaucracies, committees, and decision-trees can be a large impediment to marketing progress, a plan where decisions are made up front can eliminate much wasted time.

Yet, despite the fact that failing to perform the planning function can lead to disaster, many of us neglect this discipline. Market planning is hard work with few shortcuts. It is an easy activity to forego when more pleasant and time-sensitive tasks beckon. This is why market planning must happen at the beginning of a product introduction or budget cycle. It is very difficult to plan retroactively.

Many marketers also lack the knowledge to be effective planners. University courses on the subject offer only confusion, not enlightenment, because they approach the subject with far more complexity than is needed by the average marketing manager or business owner. Also, many courses approach market planning from a large company, product sales, media-based perspective, which is hard to adapt to situations faced by small- to mid-sized organizations, and those involved in service businesses.

Another problem with planning is that it tends to put the marketing manager on the spot. If the plan is loaded with measurable objectives (as it should be), the optimistic manager may find his own figures used against him. As Yogi Berra put it, "It's tough to make predictions, especially about the future." Many people have painfully discovered that there is a certain comfort in ambiguity. In some organizations, the penalty for missing a planned objective is so high that managers quickly learn how to play the game called "aim high and promise low."

Planning is also trickier in times of rapid change, such as those we are now facing and will continue to face in the coming years. Circumstances change so often that marketers hesitate to commit, preferring to operate by "seat-of-the-pants" methods. Although seemingly effective in the short term, this reactive management style rarely leads to long-term success.

It is also important to realize that market planning does not have to be a drawn-out, arduous process. This is true whether the organization is a small start-up company with a few thousand dollars in seed capital, or a large company with hundreds of millions or billions in assets. The basic market planning steps are the same for all organizations, even though the level of detail required varies. When in doubt, you should err on the side of simplicity, since simple plans are easier to implement.

In basic terms, the marketing plan is similar to a road map. First, you have to decide where it is you want to go; you then determine the most efficient route to take you there. Until you have this road map, it is wise to refrain from all marketing activities. This is not to say that you will always stick to the letter of the plan. Marketing plans must be constantly monitored and mid-course corrections are necessary. As Helmuth von Moltke said, *"No battle plan ever survives contact with the enemy."* However, until you have a written marketing plan as a guide, it is unwise to take your products and your promotional message to the marketplace.

Elements of the Winning Marketing Plan

There are entire texts on the subject of creating a marketing plan, and it is beyond the scope of this book to include all this information. One book I recommend is titled *Marketing Plans, How to Prepare Them, How to Use Them,* by Malcolm McDonald. Following is an outline of the elements you will want to include in your plan. You can choose to add or delete sections, but this is a good list to get you started.

SECTION I – Executive Summary or Statement of Purpose – including the scope of the plan.

SECTION II – Situation Analysis – list of all relevant facts and a brief overview of the progress (or lack of progress) your organization made in the past year.

SECTION III – Prior Year's Programs and Expenditures – also including the results you achieved.

SECTION IV – Marketing Objectives – including positioning, vertical marketing, lead generation, revenue, and public relations.

SECTION V – Creative Strategies – starting with your unique selling proposition (USP) and including the creative platform and copy themes.

SECTION VI – Target Market Identification – listing of all known market segments by product, industry, geography, company size, and any other criteria you can use as identifiers. Develop a customer profile (persona) for each of these market segments.

SECTION VII – Media and Promotional Strategies – the marketing vehicles you will use in your promotional efforts, including online, direct marketing, print, and broadcast.

SECTION VIII – Other Marketing Activities – including marketing research, trade shows and online events, public relations, collateral materials, and anything else not included in Section VII.

SECTION IX – Marketing Budget Summary – a listing of all anticipated marketing expenses by general category, summing up all the program expenses detailed in the preceding sections.

Success Tip: Spend the time necessary to complete a winning marketing plan.

Chapter 9

Measure Your Marketing Success

"I know that half of my advertising is wasted—I just don't know which half."

–John Wanamaker

Get a group of B2B marketing professionals together and ask: What are your most important criteria for benchmarking performance? You will get some blank stares and some muddled answers. However, the fact is that good marketing is both an art and a science, and unless you can explain how you and coworkers measure and report on your work output, you will not be recognized as a good marketer, let alone be viewed as an indispensable employee in a tough economic climate. Start by asking these six questions:

1. Do you have a well-defined value proposition that you communicate in all your marketing messages and promotions? Can your entire team express this message in a concise and compelling elevator pitch?

2. Is your brand/image being accepted by the marketplace? Are you seen by your prospects and customers in a way that is congruent with the way you see yourself?

3. Do you have a Service Level Agreement (SLA) with the sales department that specifies the quantity and quality of leads you will be delivering? Is this a sufficient quantity for the company to achieve its revenue objectives?

4. How many of the leads that you deliver to sales are truly qualified—by that I mean that they meet the agreed-to criteria and may actually buy something from you?

5. Are you targeting the right individuals at the right companies? Do you know who these people are and have you captured them in a system (CRM or contact database) that allows for ongoing-targeted communications?

6. Does every part of your end-to-end marketing and sales model work? Are you both effective and efficient at every phase of the process, or are there gaps that keep you from achieving your goals?

Each of these questions addresses a significant part of the value you provide to your organization. I am not saying that these should be your specific benchmark questions. However, I am saying that you need to determine and publish your own performance indicators. Remember: that which you cannot measure, you cannot improve.

Fortunately, you can measure many aspects of marketing and sales, including:

- What it costs to get an inquiry

- Percentage of inquiries that turn into leads

- Percentage of leads that turn into revenue

- Productivity of the sales force across territories/regions

- Average sales price per order

- What the marketplace thinks about you

- Your market awareness vs. your competitors

- Lifetime value of the customer

Focus on Lifetime Value

Too many marketers have a shortsighted view about objectives. They may rightly be concerned with a campaign's efficiency in generating leads or sales, and evaluate the results of each campaign in terms of the total amount of money spent and the short-term gain achieved.

By contrast, the successful marketer knows that marketing is a long-term process. He knows that the true value of each new sale is not just the immediate profit received; it is in the *lifetime value* of the new customer. He also knows it costs only one-tenth to one-fifth as much to sell a product or service to an existing customer as it does to acquire a new customer. This is why progressive organizations spend so much effort on the care and feeding of the customer, and on understanding the lifetime value of each new customer.

After calculating lifetime customer value, two things should become apparent. First, because of the long-term profit potential, most organizations should be willing to increase the amount of money they are willing to spend to acquire a new customer. Second, individual customers are more important (and profitable) than most of us realize, and should be treated accordingly.

Avoid Paralysis by Analysis

I have always found that the best marketers possess a good blend of intuition and analytic ability. While both are valuable, one of these traits without the other can be problematic. Let us look at both styles and how they can become weaknesses if not addressed appropriately.

The pure intuitive type says, "Full speed ahead—don't worry about the facts—I know how this is going to turn out." However, the fact is, few of us are born with a built-in marketing crystal ball. What some people think of as intuition is really the result of trying a lot of stuff, making mistakes, and learning about some things that generally work. One of the most humbling things you learn over the years is that your instincts about what is going to work can be faulty. Regardless of how many books you read, how many campaigns you run, or how many gray hairs you have, people can fool you sometimes.

On the other side of the spectrum are those people who practice "marketing by spreadsheet." They figure that if you just pore over the data long enough, you will learn everything you need to know to market successfully. The battle cry of these folks is, "The data, the data, give me more data." The problem is: data does not buy anything—only real people make purchases. The data can hide many important factors. Remember what the acronym GIGO stands for: Garbage In = Garbage Out. In one of my earlier books, I talked about the dangers of substandard marketing research and the many things that can cause it, including a small sample base, missing data, and a non-representative audience. Many of these same problems apply to marketing data.

The lesson is that marketing is both an art and a science, so don't rely solely on either intuition or data. You need to have a blend of both, and if you do not, concentrate on your core strength and find someone to collaborate with who can help you overcome your weaknesses. This complementary-styles approach certainly works for marriages (including my own), and it can work equally well for marketers.

Success Tip: To improve, start measuring, but do not be a victim of paralysis by analysis.

Part III
Creating an Unbeatable Positioning and Creative Strategy

Chapter 10

Develop a Powerful Positioning Strategy

"Strategy and timing are the Himalayas of marketing. Everything else is the Catskills."

– Al Ries

When I talk about *positioning*, I am referring to that place you occupy in a prospect's or customer's mind when he or she thinks about you. You may be a totally blank canvas because the prospect has never heard of you. This is not bad, because you have the opportunity to brand yourself in a fresh way. The prospect may have a negative or misinformed image of you, in which case you have some remedial work to do. On the other hand, you may occupy the position you want, and your job is one of reinforcement. Regardless of the scenario, the positioning principles are the same.

Whenever possible, I urge my clients to avoid the perception that they are a *commodity* provider. A commodity provider is one where there is no real advantage in terms of the product, service, etc., and where the prospect tends to evaluate you primarily on pricing, terms, and so forth. The alternative to being positioned on a commodity basis is to create a perception of differentiation.

I discuss a number of ways to accomplish a differentiation strategy below. You will know that you have successfully differentiated your organization when you are not in bidding wars for every piece of business and when the things that truly differentiate you are valued enough that customers are willing to pay for them. To put it another way, it is a mistake to spend a dollar in product enhancements, if your customer will only pay fifty cents more for the product.

How to Develop a Successful Positioning Strategy

The first step in developing a positioning strategy is to determine your starting point through a series of nine questions:

1. What is the scope of your positioning problem—is it to position an entire organization or simply to position a product or series of products?

2. In an ideal world, where money, time, and competitors are not a factor, what is the position you would like to hold in the marketplace?

3. What is the position that you currently hold? You must be brutally honest with the answer to this question. If you don't know the answer, conduct research to find out. This doesn't mean internal research only; you must ask prospects and customers. In many cases, employees have serious misconceptions about their company's true marketplace position.

4. What is the position of each of your competitors? How do you fit with each competitor in terms of perceived quality (including performance and functionality), service, and pricing?

5. Is the positioning statement for the current product or service compatible with your organization's overall position? As mentioned earlier, positioning consistency between the organization, products/services, and personnel is very important.

6. Does your positioning strategy violate the true nature of the organization, or is it congruent? In other words, does it ring true in every aspect? One caveat: I strongly believe in positioning yourself ahead of the curve—not just in terms of where you are now, but where you are going. But before practicing this future-oriented positioning, make sure this is where you are really going.

7. Where is the product/service in its life cycle? Is it a new, pioneering product or service, or is it in the maturing or declining phase? Do consumers ask, "What is this product?" Or do they ask, "Why should I buy this particular model from all the choices available?" Likewise, is this an opportunity to reposition a mature product for a fresh new market?

8. Do you have the resources to compete with a price strategy, by offering a product comparable to that of your competition at a lower cost?

9. Given the competition, do you have the necessary resources to reach and maintain the desired position in the marketplace? If the answer is no, you need to know this before investing marketing dollars on a failed cause.

You should answer each of these nine positioning questions in the context of overall corporate objectives, such as profit, return on investment (ROI), levels of financial risk desired, new technologies, and so forth. Note also that the questions are fairly general in nature and are intended to provide the framework in which you can develop the best possible creative strategy. The output of this process will be a position statement, which can be as short as one sentence or as long as a paragraph. Do not attempt to develop the creative strategy until you have complete agreement on the position statement from all concerned individuals, including marketing, sales, research, customer service, and finance and administration.

Proven Positioning Models

Following are examples of the different ways that an organization can be positioned. Consider these models as a starting point to establish your unique marketplace position:

Hot Company. To be considered a hot company, you must be associated with an important and current issue. Hot companies can often be found in industries such as software, health care, and medicine. Google has been a hot company for some time. But today's hot company can be tomorrow's also-ran.

Technology Leader. This works if you can reach and maintain a position of technology leadership. However, this is becoming increasingly harder to do, since new technology improvements are constantly being introduced and the life cycle for high-tech products can be as short as 12 to 18 months. So, if you wish to be a technology leader, be prepared for the constant pressure to reinvent yourself.

Warm and Fuzzy. A warm and fuzzy company builds a great deal of trust with the public and can therefore command premium prices. Examples in the consumer arena include Nordstrom and Maytag. Warm and fuzzy companies must earn this designation over time, and it can be reinforced, but not created, by advertising.

All-Knowing. This type of organization and its employees are known as the industry experts. Knowledge is America's most valuable commodity and, in service industries such as law, finance, and medicine, it is the chief differentiator among organizations. All-knowing companies can also command premium prices, particularly if they offer a strong ROI benefit to their customers.

First to Market. The first company to market a certain type of product can have a significant advantage because it can reach and gain early sales among the innovator and early adopter segments. A danger for a company positioned this way is that the second or third company will leapfrog its introduction with products that are considerably improved.

Industry Giant. The biggest company may not be the best, but it is often perceived as such. However, because of technology and re-structuring issues, the most successful organizations will be those who possess, in the words of former General Electric Chairman Jack Welch, "a big company body and a small company soul."

One and Only. If you can convince the marketplace that you are the one and only company that does something specific, particularly if that something is of significant value, your success is assured. However, the more successful you are as a one and only company, the more likely you are to attract competitors.

Fastest. Even if you're not the best, you can appeal to those who need immediate service. Distribution will be a big factor in marketing, as consumers shift dollars away from retail and toward electronic media channels. Federal Express is probably the best example of a company which was both first and fastest (with its overnight delivery service).

Cheapest. Organizations which adopt this strategy are practicing cost differentiation. Price leaders will always have a good share of the market, especially if they can combine low price with a decent quality of service (notice that I did not say a *high* quality of service). A good example of a company that does this well is Wal-Mart.

Most Personal. The ability to provide outstanding personal service can be a real differentiator, but be very careful that you can prove this over time, because such a claim is always treated with skepticism until it is proven.

Easiest to Do Business With. Many companies succeed not because of, but rather despite their selling models. A company that is easy to do business with always looks for ways to minimize anything that stands in the way of a pleasant and irritant-free experience for the customer.

Regardless of which of these positioning models you choose, or if you adopt one that is not on the list, you must present it to the consumer in a very clear and simple manner. It should also be focused and consistent, since it is difficult to sell more than one concept at a time.

Success Tip: Choose a positioning model that is compelling and sustainable.

Chapter 11

Establish a Strong Creative Platform

"Creativity is the power to connect the seemingly unconnected."

–William Plomer

I recommend that you develop a creative platform before you generate any promotions or advertisements. The creative platform will ensure that you have done your homework and that you achieve consistency in your messaging and graphics. It will also make it easier to come up with practical creative ideas that actually achieve their intended purpose.

Here are the questions to ask to ensure that you create a strong and compelling creative platform. Make sure that you invite those who are outside the marketing organization, including sales, product development, and customer support.

- What do you want your marketing programs to accomplish? What problem are you trying to solve? How do you intend your advertising and promotional strategy to support the organization's position statement?

- Who is your primary target audience? What are their needs and interests?

- What is the most important benefit of your product or service to its primary and secondary audiences? What are the second and third most important benefits?

- How can you prove your product or service claims? If you are selling a product or service that claims a cost benefit, how can you prove the return on investment (ROI)? This information will be necessary for the copy that supports the headline statements.

- What is your offer? What exactly are you going to give the prospect for her money? You must pay careful attention to the offer, because it is second in importance only to the choice of the target audience.

- Who is your competition? What are their perceived and actual areas of differentiation? What is their marketing strategy and where are they running their promotions? If you were in the competitor's place, what would you do to beat you?

- What is your unique selling proposition (USP)? How have you added value that is different from what the customer can receive from your competition?

- What are the consequences if the prospect decides to do nothing—to not make a purchase?

- What is the size of the marketing budget? Do you have the necessary resources to overcome the competition and achieve your positioning objectives? If the answer to this question is no, then you must either reset the objectives or re-calibrate the budget. Better to do this now than later.

Elements of a Creative Platform

Give each of the above questions thorough consideration to help develop your creative platform. Use the structure below to organize a written document that you can share with anyone who is creating promotions and advertisements. The purpose of the creative platform document is not to give you extra work—rather it is to help you organize your thoughts to create a powerhouse campaign that meets or beats the objectives.

1. The scope of the campaign – State the problem you are trying to solve with this particular campaign or promotion.

2. Target audience – Talk about the prospects you are trying to reach in terms of industries, titles, size of company, and any other factors that define your primary and secondary audience segments.

3. Specific objectives of the campaign – State whether you are trying to generate awareness, leads, or revenue, and the measurable yardsticks of accomplishment. Describe the behavior you will influence in terms of exactly what you want the prospect to do.

4. Benefits of your product or service – List the attributes of your brand and state how these characteristics bring major benefits to the customer. Describe the specifics of the offer.

5. The major selling idea – Talk about the uniqueness of your offer and the most important reasons why prospects will engage with you or buy your product.

6. Competition – Describe the alternatives to the pros-

pect engaging with you and discuss what your competition offers that you do not.

7. Creative theme – Write about how your message, product/service story and offer will convince the prospect to take action.

8. Brand and creative components – Talk about how your branding will be presented and discuss design components, copy tone and voice, use of graphics, photography, etc.

The Importance of the Elevator Pitch

In case you have not heard of the concept, an elevator pitch is an attention-grabbing and engaging message you can share with someone when faced with limited time (thirty to sixty seconds)—i.e., the amount of time you have between floors in an elevator. Here is the three-part formula on how to construct an elevator pitch, courtesy of Robert W. Bly, one of the world's premier copywriters (and a prolific author):

1. Do you know how...? (fill in the blank with a problem your audience can identify with).

2. What we do is... (explain what you do that solves their problem).

3. This allows you to.... (state the benefits achieved by using your product or service).

As an example, here is an elevator pitch for a company that supplies content management software: "You know how companies have trouble managing their documents and have costly and inefficient workflow processes? What we do is securely manage those documents and provide simple workflow tools to streamline business processes. This allows companies to save huge amounts of time, money, and aggravation."

Note that you should write this elevator pitch in a conversational tone, and not in the manner you would write it for a press release or company brochure. The point is to first express the pain point that the individual can identify with, and then get the key benefits into his or her mind in the shortest amount of time. A few tips for constructing your elevator pitch:

- Remember that the audience is the prospect, not an industry insider, so keep the technical jargon to a minimum.

- Acronyms usually confuse more than enlighten.

- Have everyone in your company, and especially your marketing and sales staffs, memorize the elevator pitch.

- One or two memorable points are better than cramming in too much information.

Let's face it—we are living in an "elevator world." The majority of your prospects are distracted. Use this formula to construct a great elevator pitch to break through the distractions.

Success tip: Use the creative platform and elevator pitch to develop powerful marketing campaigns.

Chapter 12

Write Copy That Produces Results

"Good communication is as stimulating as black coffee and just as hard to sleep after."

– Anne Morrow Lindbergh

Even experienced marketers find the subject of writing copy confusing and intimidating. I will clear up some of the mystery and show you how to use proven formulas to organize the writing process. There are dozens of books and hundreds of articles on the art of writing copy, each with its own unique viewpoint. Certain authors would have you believe that writing copy is like painting by numbers, saying something like "Just follow ten easy steps and wait for the orders to come pouring in." If life could only be that easy!

Writing winning promotional copy is getting tougher for several reasons. Competition is fierce, since we are all forced to compete for a slow-growing number of prospects. Consumers are better educated, more sophisticated, more aware of promotional strategies, and less likely to fall for hype or gross exaggeration. Advertising clutter is everywhere, and prospects are exposed to hundreds of advertising claims daily, very few of which are actually targeted to their individual needs and desires. The good news is that each of these problems leads to its own opportunity. Good copy can definitely help your organization compete successfully for your prospect's attention and dollars.

How to Be a Great Communicator

You build successful copywriting upon a foundation of good communication and you must be willing to accept 100 percent responsibility for the quality and acceptance of your message. It is your burden to ensure that your prospect not only hears, but also understands the message, in exactly the way you intended. And you must do this on your prospect's terms, not your terms.

Always keep in mind that the prospect owes you nothing. He or she has no obligation to listen to you or even acknowledge your existence. Your challenge is to convince these preoccupied individuals, one at a time, to make your organization and its product or service the most important thing in their lives, at least for a few brief moments. This is a humbling and important task.

So how do you know if you are being a good communicator of the corporate message? Whether you write your own copy or use an outside resource, you need to be able to judge its effectiveness. Good communication should always meet five criteria:

1. The message achieves its stated objective, whether that objective is to sell products, generate leads, acquire new members, or improve your organization's image. The good copywriter always keeps his "eyes on the prize."

2. It is targeted at the correct audience. You must thoroughly understand your audience to write good copy. Amateurs write copy first and then ask if it fits the audience. The true professional asks many questions about the audience before developing creative themes.

3. The copy forwards your cause. The advertisement should make friends for your organization, not lose them. This means that you should not follow a short-term strategy of hyperbole and exaggerations, or deliberately mislead your audience. Nor should you write *shock value* copy. Yes, it would bring you attention, but it rarely pays off in the long-term.

4. It is memorable. No copywriter can attain immortality, but the closest one can come is to create advertisements that so capture the imaginations of the audience that they are remembered long after the promotions have stopped running.

5. It is unique. In a world full of *me-too* advertising, fresh, vibrant copy will always stand out. Response rates for almost all industries have dropped to the point where the cookie cutter approach does not produce adequate results. Being different does have its risks, but it also offers the greatest rewards.

Before You Sit Down to Write

As a great admirer of Wolfgang Amadeus Mozart, I have always been intrigued by how he was able to create such beautiful music. Mozart credited much of his success to his in-depth musical training as a child. In fact, Mozart never stopped studying music until his untimely death at the age of thirty-five. One of the amazing things about Mozart is that he first composed his works in his mind, and then simply recorded the notes on paper. He rarely had to change a manuscript once it was written. Mozart kept no copies of the original score because he could always reconstruct the manuscript from memory.

I have often pondered (frequently over the sixth draft of something) how wonderful it must be to have such a talent. Unfortunately, the fact is that such genius is in very short supply, and most of us find writing to be a difficult and tedious process.

If you can afford to hire a qualified writer, I highly recommend that you do so. However, if your budget doesn't allow for this, you must prepare yourself for the task. The best preparation for writing is in-depth knowledge of your product or service, backed up by a well-conceived offer. I suggest you spend a greater percentage of your time in the up-front disciplines of research and offer development. While these are not the glamorous parts of the writing process, the extra preparation will make your copy more effective and much easier to write.

After conducting research and developing the offer, you should list every benefit you can think of for your product or service. When you are sure you have an exhaustive list, rank these benefits in the order that you perceive them to be important to your prospects. Your goal is to locate and stress the single most important benefit, plus two or three secondary benefits to emphasize throughout the copy.

Remember that when you are developing the offer, ranking benefits, or writing copy, you should always be thinking of one individual, not a group of nameless, faceless prospects. If you are someone who cringes at the thought that your writing will be read by thousands of individuals, then you will definitely benefit from this technique.

This method of focusing on one individual is often taught in public speaking classes as a cure for nervousness. Speakers are taught to pick out a few friendly faces in the crowd, and act as if they are speaking only to these people. I have done this myself. The technique is easily transferable to copywriting, by visualizing one prospect and then writing copy for that specific individual. In fact, it helps if you speak about your product to someone who fits the profile of the target audience. Then, write something that you believe would capture your prospect's attention and persuade that particular individual to accept your offer.

Useful Copywriting Formulas

To help you get your thoughts on paper (or preferably, computer), it helps to have a formula. One of the better-known and time-tested copywriting formulas is AIDA. It works well and is easy to remember.

The first "A" in AIDA stands for *Attention*. You must always capture your prospect's attention as a first step in convincing him to respond affirmatively to your offer. Without gaining attention, there is no sale. Depending on the media used, attention-getting devices can include bold benefit statements, curiosity-provoking questions, strong graphic images, giveaway offers, official looking formats, and many others.

The "I" in AIDA stands for *Interest*. Once you have captured a prospect's attention you must then arouse her interest in hearing more about your product or service. Many sales are lost at the border between attention and interest. One technique for building interest is to open your copy with strong benefit statements. Sales trainers teach the concept of selling benefits, not features, and this concept is equally valid in promotional copy.

The "D" in AIDA stands for *Desire*. After you have captured the prospect's attention and built interest in your product or service – you must then convince the prospect that what you are offering is worth more than what she will have to give you in return. This is known as *proving the value equation*. Remember that you must prove the value equation by building a strong case for the value of your product or service as it relates to a specific prospect.

The final "A" in AIDA stands for *Action*. This is where you give your prospect sufficient motivation to send in the lead form, go online to register, or pick up the phone and call. Since you have been building the motivation to respond from the beginning of the advertisement, the favorable action of the prospect should be the logical conclusion to the process.

Just as it is important to lead the prospect to say YES, you must never give him a reason to say NO. Terms should be clear and the Web form or order coupon should be easy to read and fill out. It is also advisable to restate the major benefit and guarantees.

PAPA is another easy-to-remember formula for writing copy in various media. Its letters stand for Promise, Amplify, Proof, and Action.

Promise – Use the headline to promise the reader or listener a significant benefit which your product or service provides.

Amplify – After the promise is made, it should be covered in as much detail as possible. Amplification can include secondary benefits, product features, and product specifications.

Proof – Even after the promise has been made and amplified, you must convince a skeptical prospect that your organization is legitimate, that your product will do exactly what you claim it will do, or that your service will be performed to the customer's specifications. There are three basic methods of establishing this proof: product usage demonstrations, testimonials, and satisfaction guarantees.

Action – As with the AIDA formula, everything you do or say must lead the reader or listener to take action. You must tell the prospect, in specific and understandable terms, how and where to take advantage of your offer.

A Selling Formula that Works In Copywriting

I have spent over two and a half decades as a marketing professional, but have also had several opportunities to manage sales organizations. Although they are handled at different sides of the process, marketing and personal selling have a great deal in common. Good salespeople follow a series of steps that are designed to conclude in a purchase decision. They learn that each step is critical and must be followed in sequence (with flexibility of course) to achieve the desired outcome. Likewise, each of these selling steps has its equivalent procedure in promotional copy.

Step One – Create an atmosphere of credibility. You can achieve credibility with social media, image advertising, public relations, and mass-marketing techniques. The object is to predispose the prospect to accept your offer, whether it is the next time he sees your product in a catalog or the next time he receives an email offer from you at the office.

Step Two – Establish rapport. People prefer to buy from someone they like. This is why a salesperson will quickly find common ground with a prospect, such as shared hobbies or mutual friends. Advertisers build rapport with warm and inviting graphics and copy, while online and direct marketers build rapport by knowing their customers and using database techniques to appeal to their unique characteristics.

Step Three – Grab attention. The number one tool salespeople use to grab attention is the strong benefit statement, *Mr. Prospect, my product will give you fifty percent more output at the same cost.* Likewise, marketers lead from strength by opening with the primary benefit, or a curiosity-provoking headline.

Step Four – Support the benefit statement. This is the "prove it" stage. Salespeople prove it with product demonstrations and lists of product features. Marketers prove it with demonstrations, user testimonials, and money-back satisfaction guarantees.

Step Five – Overcome objections. Sales trainers teach their pupils a series of answers to common prospect objections. Since the marketer may not have the ability to personally respond to a spoken objection, he must learn to anticipate potential objections and answer them within the advertisement, online offer, or direct mail package.

Step Six – Close the sale. Whether face-to-face, as in personal selling, or through a marketing offer, it all comes down to closing the sale. A good salesperson asks for the order repeatedly. Marketers should be equally bold in asking for the order. Both must tell the prospects exactly what to do—buy the product.

Importance of the Emotional Appeal

Whether you use the AIDA formula, the PAPA formula, or any other process for writing copy, you must keep one important point in mind: *Logic follows emotion.* Writers who approach the copy process by attempting to logically prove the merits of their product or service are making a big mistake. The fact is, most individuals make the buying decision for emotional reasons first, and then look for logical arguments to justify the decision they have already made. So always look for ways to "Lead with the heart, and follow with the brain."

> ***Success Tip:*** Follow a proven formula to write compelling promotional copy.

Chapter 13

Drive Action with a Compelling Offer

"Marketing has one purpose: to sell more stuff to more people more often for more money more efficiently."

— Sergio Zyman

Assuming that you have a quality product or service, with a compelling value proposition, aimed at the right target audience, the offer will be a key difference in your success (or lack thereof). So what do I mean by *offer*? In simple terms, an offer is what you propose to give to the prospect, and what you are asking for in return. The offer is the "What's in it for me?" part of the marketing equation. How do you know if you have an effective offer? Here are the six criteria every business-to-business offer should meet:

1. It works. Unless the offer achieves the intended results, it is not a good offer.

2. It is compatible with your organization's positioning statement. Offers that are not compatible may generate short-term results but be counterproductive in the long term.

3. It is compelling enough to cut through the marketplace clutter and your prospect's preoccupation. The average consumer is exposed to up to 3,000 promotional messages per week. You must have an offer that stands out clearly to overcome this barrage.

4. It is targeted at exactly the right audience. For instance, employees are motivated by offers that help them get promoted, build their work spheres of influence, and make their jobs easier or faster. Upper management is motivated by increased sales, lower costs, and saving time.

5. It is aimed at the proper stage of the sales cycle. For example, information offers are used for prospects that are in the information-gathering stage, and pricing offers are used when prospects are in the purchasing phase.

6. It is powerful enough to demand immediate attention from the prospect. If possible, the offer should be tied to a strong call to action that shouts, "Take advantage of this offer right now."

Types of Offers

Although by no means inclusive, here are some examples of offers that work for business-to-business products and services:

Straight Sale – The straight sale offer is basically an exchange of product or service for money, with no added inducement. Given all the other possibilities, this is a relatively weak type of offer.

Special Pricing – This offer works well with later-stage prospects who already know about your product or service. The special pricing offer could be a discount for prompt action or an urge to "buy now before the price goes up."

Introductory Offer – An introductory offer is used to introduce new prospects to your company. It will have the greatest effect when the discount is significant. You have to be careful, however, not to offend existing customers who just purchased the same product for more money than you charge new buyers.

Multiple Product – With this offer, buyers get the second or subsequent products at no charge, or at a large discount.

Premium – Something extra is given away to spur the prospect to purchase now. Premiums range from advertising specialties such as desk calendars and pens, to expensive items such as trips and electronic equipment.

Free Information – Similar to the premium offer, but you give away information instead of a product. This is especially effective with a business audience, since people are always interested in ways to save money and perform their jobs better. Plus, this type of offer can often be fulfilled immediately via a computer download.

Trade-in or Trade-up Offer – The prospect trades in an old item and gets a discount on the new item. For example, a computer manufacturer can give businesses that trade in a competitor's equipment a $500 credit toward the purchase of a new computer. This way you meet two objectives: sell a product and displace the competitor.

Free Trial – If you have confidence in your product, let potential customers try it out in their office for thirty days. This has been a strong offer for software companies, equipment manufacturers, and publishers.

Satisfaction Guarantee – While a guarantee should be part of every offer, an extra-strong guarantee can serve as its own offer. An example would be "double your money back if not completely satisfied."

Send a Salesperson – This works for only the most qualified leads: those who are ready, willing, and able to buy. You must be careful with this offer (or offer a less threatening alternative as well) since it will scare off many lukewarm prospects.

Cash Discount – A special price can be given to help force the purchase decision. This offer works well in combination with free trial offers. The prospect has the option to try the product and pay full price if he decides to keep it, or pay for the product now and receive a substantial discount.

Special Terms – This can work as well as a cash discount. For instance, "receive the item now and take up to six months to pay with no interest." In some cases, purchasers will be more interested in the monthly payment terms than the total cash amount.

Sweepstakes – With this offer, any prospect who replies to your offer is automatically entered into a prize drawing. Due to state and federal regulations, you will probably not be able to restrict the sweepstakes to purchasers only, but the offer still works because many people think they have a better chance of winning if they order something.

Demo/Trial Offer – A smaller, trial version of the product is sent (sometimes for a fee, sometimes for free). If the prospect likes the demo, he orders the full product. This offer works well for computer software products and publications.

Free Samples – Free samples are an effective way to highlight your product. For instance, an office product manufacturer can offer day planners or desk lamps as a bonus for purchasing a desk set.

Performance Guarantee – The customer gets to use the product for a period of time. If it does not live up to the specified criteria, she can return it for a full refund. This offer works well if your product is clearly superior to its competition.

Special Inducement – Something extra is given to the prospect if he acts immediately. The inducement could be extra product, better terms, free training, or extended maintenance.

The type of offer you use should be based on the objectives of your program. If you are selling a high-ticket or complex product, or if you need to make a personal sales call to finalize a transaction, you should choose an offer geared to generating leads. Conversely, if you are promoting a low-ticket, non-complex item via online, phone, or mail, you will use a different type of offer.

Success Tip: Work hard at developing and testing offers.

Chapter 14

Motivate Your Prospects to Action

"Motivation is the art of getting people to do what you want them to do because they want to do it."

– Dwight David Eisenhower

Successful creative strategies are not those that are clever, win awards, sound really interesting, or get people to pay attention. All of these outcomes are desirable, but they are not the reason we marketers should spend so much time thinking about our creative platform. Rather, our goal is to drive action. That action may come in a one-step process—where the prospect sees the promotion and buys immediately, or it may be in a series of steps beginning with creating awareness; but in the end, we earn our keep by transforming prospects into customers.

To become a master at generating buying actions, it helps to understand exactly what it is that causes people to buy. And it probably won't surprise you that people buy products and services to satisfy the same needs and desires that they attempt to satisfy with many of their other daily choices. Whether it is Mr. Joe Consumer buying from home, or Ms. Sally Business Owner purchasing for her company, consumers buy for the following reasons:

- To solve a problem

- To increase knowledge

- To feel more comfortable

- To make life easier

- To become more valuable

- To satisfy a curiosity

- To feel better about themselves

Very few people go through a checklist when deciding to make a purchase, but there is in fact an unstated process. First, they must have a perceived need or desire (not necessarily a genuine need or desire) for what you offer. Then they have to believe that your offering satisfies their requirements, and they must also be convinced that you are trustworthy and your claims are believable.

To put it another way, prospects have to be satisfied with the basic value proposition—that what they receive by doing business with you is worth as much, or more, than what you are asking them to spend (including money, time, and effort). Finally, they must believe that the risk of doing business with you is low or manageable.

As I explained in the chapter on copywriting, people buy with emotion and justify their purchases with logic. This is why advertising that appeals to the emotions is often more successful than that which appeals to logic. So first make your appeal to the emotional side of the prospect, then give him or her lots of good, logical fact-based reasons to justify the decision already emotionally made. To express this in another way: first sell to the heart, and then the head.

One more thing to keep in mind—your job as a Fusion Marketer is not just to differentiate your product or service from your competitors.

Whether making a small purchase or a big-ticket item, people often have some degree of fear and anxiety when approaching the buying process. If the experience is anything but pleasant, the prospect is ready to revert to the status quo, make do with what he or she already has, and either delay or decide to forego the purchase altogether. How many of us neglect to go shopping for the new car, or that new software program, because we just do not want to deal with a time-consuming and hassle-filled buying experience?

Your job as a marketing or sales professional is to negate or overcome this fear and anxiety by making the shopping and purchasing experience as painless as possible. This can, in fact, be a point of competitive differentiation. Two of the most important buying motivations are to make life easier and to feel more comfortable, so whatever you can do to help your prospects achieve these objectives will be well rewarded.

Motivational Appeals That Work

Napoleon Bonaparte said, *"There are two levers for moving men: interest and fear."* These are indeed the two master motivators, and all others are a subset of these behavioral drivers. Because we humans can be motivated in a surprising variety of ways, using the correct incentive (including message and offer) for a specific audience is a hallmark of good marketing. Here are examples of appeals that have proven successful for many different types of products.

Greed – Everyone is susceptible to greed to some degree. While greed is usually thought of as a negative emotion, it is really just the desire to get a better deal than the next person, or to enhance our position at a low cost. Copywriters who effectively push the greed button sell a lot of products.

Fear, Uncertainty, and Doubt (FUD) – With the FUD formula, you are selling from the negative perspective. Instead of saying "If you buy our product, these good things will happen to you," FUD copy implies, "If you don't buy our product, these bad things will happen to you." Fear has been used in financial marketing to persuade prospects that their current investments are suspect, and in the computer industry to convince prospects that their current technology has shortcomings that leave them in a weak competitive posture.

Guilt – Although you need to use it carefully, guilt can be a powerful motivation tool. A good example of this type of appeal is AT&T's successful "reach out and touch someone" campaign that ran from 1979 to 1983, and was resurrected in 2003. The campaign's not-so-subtle theme is that you should feel guilty for not calling your loved ones (especially your mother) when AT&T makes it so convenient.

Curiosity – This appeal is most effective with so-called early adopters of products. Some people have a strong need to own, or at least know about, the newest products and services. If you have the task of generating leads for a new product or service, create the curiosity in your advertising by withholding a little information. A curiosity-seeker who is satisfied does not respond to advertising.

Status or Exclusivity – People who have children know this as the reverse psychology approach. As soon as you tell your child he can't have something, his interest in the forbidden object increases dramatically. Likewise, for many individuals, the desirability of a product rises in direct proportion to its difficulty of attainment.

Time Pressure – This appeal works better in a supporting role. Time pressure creates a sense of urgency by saying "buy me today because it will cost you more tomorrow" or "only the first 200 respondents can take advantage of this offer."

Convenience – Most people (me included) feel a great deal of time pressure in their lives. Marketers who show people how their products and services will save them time and/or make their lives easier (at work or at home) have a significant selling benefit.

Financial – The financial hot buttons of your prospects can be pushed two ways: first, by demonstrating how your product or service will save money, and second, by demonstrating how your product or service will help generate more income.

Learning – Many people have a thirst for knowledge and this can be a strong appeal in your promotional copy. They want information on how to do their jobs better, make their companies more profitable, and have a successful business and home life.

One important aspect to remember about the two master motivation levers: While fear can be a strong short-term motivator, interest (positive rewards) is usually more effective for long-term changes. This is equally true whether you are trying to get your children to do the right things, or to get your prospects to make a purchase.

Success Tip: Choose the motivator that most appeals to your target audience.

Part IV

Aligning Marketing and Sales for Super Success

Chapter 15

Choose the Best Marketing and Sales Model

"Strategy is choosing to run a different race because it's the one you've set yourself up to win."

– Michael Porter, Harvard Business School

It bears repeating that despite all the possible permutations of how you can get there, there are only three ways to grow your business:

1. Increase the number of customers

2. Increase the average transaction size

3. Increase the frequency of purchase

In order to be successful, you must align your marketing and sales model to meet one or more of these three objectives. If you can increase all three metrics, you will soon have a world-class operation. And while there are many possible ways to achieve a revenue objective, some organizations (perhaps yours) are not using the best strategy. Each of the possible methods has its plusses and minuses, and the best choice for you is not always the obvious choice. You should not make decisions regarding your marketing and sales model simply based on what your competitors are doing, but rather on your unique assets and weaknesses.

Tough Questions that You Need to Answer

Before considering embarking on a new way of doing business, it is helpful to understand your current situation. Begin by asking seven questions:

1. How did your current marketing and sales model evolve?

2. What is your motivation for keeping the status quo?

3. Are you doing things out of habit or by deliberate choice?

4. Is your sales force earning its keep?

5. Are your current channel partners helping or hindering progress?

6. Where is the Pareto Principle (80/20) alive and well in your organization?

7. Are there any *time bombs* at your company?

Time bombs are those issues that, if not addressed, could have serious consequences downstream. If you prefer a different analogy, think of time bombs as the potential Achilles tendons of your organization—where you are most vulnerable to atrophy or attack. Remember the Andy Grove statement I mentioned earlier: "Only the paranoid survive." Fusion Marketers know the best time to be paranoid is when you don't feel that you have to be. Here are a few of the most insidious time bombs:

• A cost of sales that is out of control.

- Good products but a sales team that is stable, comfortable, and very inefficient.

- Channel partners that are leaving you for the competition.

- A prohibitive cost-of-goods.

- Products that are more than one generation behind the competition.

Acceptance and the Courage to Change

A very smart theologian named Reinhold Niebuhr wrote something that we now refer to as the Serenity Prayer around seventy years ago: "God, give us grace to accept with serenity the things that cannot be changed, courage to change the things that should be changed, and the wisdom to distinguish the one from the other." This wisdom can be applied to many parts of our lives, including how we conduct business. And when it comes to things we cannot change, there are five that are most important to establishing the right sales model:

1. You cannot make bad sales reps into good sales reps. Okay, there may be a few exceptions, but generally, if you have underperforming reps, you will need to face the situation and get some new ones.

2. You cannot turn weak channel partners into strong performers. Just as with hiring sales reps, the secret is to find and motivate the good channel partners.

3. Sales reps and channel partners always "follow the money." A weak compensation plan will lead to weak sales. As one shrewd sales VP told me: "Sales reps are coin-operated. They always follow the money."

4. Sometimes you need to tweak the model, and sometimes you need to totally change the model. This is where the "courage to change" part comes in. Holding on to a weak sales model is just postponing the inevitable day of reckoning.

5. Unless you are in a rare monopoly situation, customers have control, not you. This is where the "accepting" part comes in. The trick is to figure out your organizational strengths and align these strengths with the way customers desire to do business.

There are three steps in the alignment process:

1. Survey how your customers buy now and how they want to buy in the future: sales rep, distributor, retail, Web, mail order, telephone, etc.

2. Align the key buying criteria with the ability of each selling model to fulfill specific criteria.

3. Offer flexibility as your customers change their needs/ wants.

Comparing Sales Models

Now that you have asked the tough questions and researched potential time bombs, it is time to explore the various marketing and selling models. The chart below will help you to understand the options.

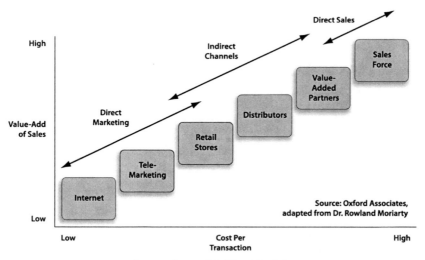

Comparison of Selling Models

There are two major factors and five minor factors to take into consideration when choosing a marketing and sales model. The major factors are the two values illustrated in the above chart: the cost to complete each transaction and the value that each transaction brings to the business. It is not surprising that the direct sales force is both the highest cost and highest value option. At the other end of the continuum is Internet (Web-based) selling, where the costs can be very low, but the average sales size also tends to be low. The best situation is to have a high-value transaction facilitated with low-cost marketing and sales techniques. Conversely, the worst situation is to have a low-value transaction created using high-cost techniques (e.g., partners or direct sales). The overall objective is to drive the highest average transaction cost at the lowest cost-per-sales.

The other factors to take into consideration when considering your choice of sales model are:

The degree of commoditization – Are you selling a product or service that is standardized and familiar to the audience? Is it something that others are selling, where the main differentiation is not in the product or service, but rather in the price or delivery method?

Degree of complexity – Is your offering easy to understand, or does it require a lot of hand-holding and training? Can others grasp it quickly?

Amount of customization required – Is the product or service always delivered in the same way, or does it require special services like customization or configuration?

Level of maturity – Is your product or service stable, or is it still in the developmental stage?

Customer risk – Do customers feel they are taking a chance in buying your product or service, or do they feel secure because of the stability and maturity of the company and the product?

Direct, Channel and Hybrid Models

Here are some instances where a pure direct sales model usually works best:

- When you have solid geographic coverage.

- When you sell big-ticket (costly) products.

- When you sell complex products.

- When you have the funds to sustain a sales force through the start-up period.

- When you cannot afford to heavily discount your products.

- When a high cost-of-goods makes paying a channel margin prohibitive.

A pure channel sales model usually works best:

- When you can readily identify potential resellers who know your industry.

- When you have limited people to cover a geographic area.

- When you need specific vertical or horizontal expertise.

- When you have a relatively low cost-of-goods.

There are also circumstances when a mixed or hybrid direct and channel model works best:

- When you have a mix of geographic coverage.

- When your customer mix includes a blend of small and large companies.

- When you need the vertical/domain expertise that a channel brings.

- When the economics work for both models.

In the hybrid model, direct or field sales people focus on large and profitable accounts, complex sales, quality (not quantity), upgrading and cross-selling accounts, and becoming customer advocates. The following chart illustrates the differences in account coverage in the direct and hybrid models.

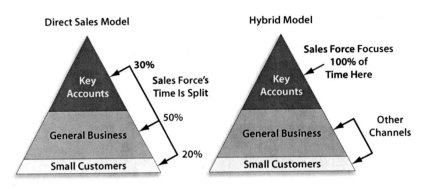

Source: The Channel Advantage

Even if you decide the pure channel model is preferable for your company, it is a good idea to first establish the ability to sell directly. You will gain extremely valuable information about your marketplace, value proposition, price points, and so forth.

Success Tip: No matter how painful, be prepared to change a sales model that is not working.

Chapter 16

Build a Powerful Lead Engine

"In order for any business to succeed, it must first become a system, so that the business functions exactly the same way every time...down to the very last detail."
                                    –Michael Gerber, The E Myth

This chapter assumes that you are using two or more steps to close business, starting with the generation of an inquiry or lead. If you sell as a one-step process, skip this chapter and read on.

In a typical business-to-business scenario, responses you generate will flow through the marketing system and during the end-to-end process will fall into the following categories:

1. Database Build – Contact names you have added to your database who have not responded to a promotional offer. You collect these names for remarketing purposes because they match the prospect criteria. Your mission is to turn them into raw inquiries.

2. Raw Inquiry – Any person/company that responds to one of your marketing promotions, from any source,

whether qualified or not. Your mission is to turn raw inquires into suspects or qualified leads.

3. Suspect – An inquiry that has passed your initial screening and is deemed to have some potential to become a customer. Your mission is to turn suspects into qualified leads.

4. Qualified Lead – A lead that has gone through a more in-depth qualification process, either by filling out a Web lead form or by being asked a series of questions by a sales development rep. At this point, the lead may be classified as a hot prospect (one ready to make a decision), a warm prospect (one with the capacity to become a hot prospect), a suspect, or a dead lead.

5. Inactive Lead – This is a person who will not buy now, but who you deem to have potential for the future. You should enter these leads into your database system and continue to remarket to them until they become suspects or qualified leads.

6. Dead Lead – This lead has no chance of becoming a customer. But be careful in assigning leads to the *dead file*. So-called dead leads can often be resurrected and become purchasers. In fact, some companies assign new salespeople to work the dead lead file, often with surprising success. You should also put your competitors in the dead lead file so that you can exclude them from future marketing efforts.

7. Opportunity – An opportunity is a lead that has been qualified and is being worked in an active sales cycle,

with a potential dollar amount assigned. Best practice is to only let sales reps classify a lead as an opportunity.

8. Customer – If you have done your job properly, a fair percentage of raw inquiries have been worked through the system and have become customers. Now your job is to get them to buy more products or services.

9. Repeat Customer – The lifeblood of any business. Most companies devote too few resources to increasing revenues from existing customers, even though the cost to bring in an additional dollar of revenue from an existing client is far less than the cost of generating a dollar from a new customer.

How to Turn Leads into Customers

Think of the end-to-end marketing and sales process as an assembly line. You need to carefully monitor every step of the process, from generating raw inquiries through building repeat clients. Formulas called *conversion ratios* are used to measure what percentage of leads survive each step and move closer to becoming customers. If your conversion ratios are on target, your entire program will produce the intended results. But just like any process on the assembly line, if any of your conversion ratios are out of whack, overall output is negatively impacted.

For example, if you generate 100 raw leads from a particular marketing program, and fifty survive the initial screening step to earn the designation *suspect*, the conversion ratio of raw leads to suspects is fifty percent. Likewise, if twenty of these fifty suspects are turned into qualified leads, the conversion ratio of suspects to qualified leads is forty percent. And if five of these twenty prospects become customers, the conversion ratio of prospects to customers is twenty-five percent.

Conversion ratios will differ depending on your industry, the product or service, the type of prospects with whom you are working, and such factors as seasonality and the economy. The important point is to work and rework these numbers to increase the conversion ratio at each step. After you have a handle on your realistic ratios, you will know exactly how many raw leads need to be fed into the system on an ongoing basis to achieve your sales objectives.

By using conversion ratios, it is easy to demonstrate that a company can use its lead generation system to increase the number of new customers in three ways. Option one is to funnel a larger number of raw leads into the system, while maintaining the same conversion ratios. Option two is to improve one or more of the conversion ratios, while maintaining the same number of raw leads entering the system. Option three is to do both.

Whenever I use the Fusion Marketing methods to evaluate a company's lead generation program (or help them create a new marketing and sales machine), I first look for the underperforming parts of the process (weaknesses in the assembly line) and then help them fix these areas to create a well-oiled lead engine.

As I discuss elsewhere, it is important that marketing and sales establish a service level agreement (SLA) that quantifies:

- Number of qualified leads required

- Time period in which these leads will be generated

- Criteria of qualified leads

- Pipeline coverage needed to meet sales objectives

You need to negotiate the specific lead engine numbers as well as the specifics of what constitutes a qualified lead. For example, some companies might consider a B2B lead to be qualified if it meets these four attributes:

1. There is an established project at the company that could potentially use the type of product or service you offer.

2. The project is budgeted.

3. The project is to be delivered in a reasonably short time frame (e.g., less than six months).

4. You have access to the decision-maker.

As for pipeline coverage, it is important to discover how many potential dollars of revenue you need in active sales engagements to achieve a specific amount of revenue. As I mentioned above, to be considered an *opportunity* there must be a dollar amount of potential revenue assigned. Over time, you will find that your company needs X amount of total dollars in the pipeline to generate Y amount of revenue. For example, if you find that your sales reps need to be working $4 million worth of opportunities to achieve $1 million of revenue, then your pipeline to sales ratio is 4 to 1. Remember that this is another conversion ratio and if you can lower this ratio to 3 to 1, then the same $4 million in the pipeline will lead to $1.33 million in revenue. Unlike their less-informed counterparts, Fusion Marketers understand the basics of sales forecasting and pipeline management.

Criteria of a Powerful Lead Generation Engine

Even the most creative branding and awareness building program will not produce the desired results unless you can efficiently work prospects through the system and produce revenue at the other end. Therefore, you should continually evaluate your lead generation program to ensure that it meets these seven criteria:

1. You use conversion ratios to continually monitor re-

sults at every step of the process and to refine the lead program to produce greater results.

2. The system produces a high percentage of qualified leads.

3. You follow up all leads, except those that are obviously unqualified.

4. You contact all leads by email, phone, mail, or a personal visit, in a timely manner (preferably within 24 hours).

5. The inbound lead flow is balanced by territory, sales reps, and product line.

6. You produce inquiries/leads at a reasonable average cost.

7. You capture all information generated from inquiries and subsequent follow-up immediately (and preferably automatically) in a database system.

One of the great benefits of creating an efficient lead engine is that it will allow you to precisely measure your cost of acquisition. When you know what it costs to bring in a new customer, you can then focus on lowering this cost while simultaneously increasing the average sale amount. By manipulating these two levers, you can vastly increase your company's success.

Whatever your product or service, never underestimate the importance of a well-tuned lead generating program. Since three out of every four business-to-business marketing communications are for lead generation purposes, you should put focused and professional attention in an area that is so vital to your success.

Nurture Leads with Friendly Persistence

Because it takes an average of seven or eight contacts to turn a raw inquiry into a customer (and sometimes many more contacts), you should put a lot of emphasis on nurturing every inquiry in your database. Many companies make a huge mistake by discarding or ignoring leads if they fail to buy or engage with you after two or three attempts. Do not be one of these companies. As a Fusion Marketer, you need to aggressively market to your database of prospects until each person or company in the database takes some positive action, or until you disqualify them as a legitimate prospect.

The pie-chart below shows an average distribution of inbound inquiries from B2B marketing programs. Eight percent (labeled as A Leads) are qualified prospects that are actively looking for a product or service. Seven percent (labeled as B Leads) are qualified prospects with a mid-term need. Thirty percent (labeled as F Leads) are disqualified, now and in the future. But it is the way you handle the other fifty-five percent (labeled as C Leads) of inactive leads that will determine your success. Keep in mind that thirty percent or more of C leads will eventually make a purchase, which represents a greater volume of business than the A and B leads combined. So do put a lot of effort into closing the A and B leads but also put equal effort into nurturing and qualifying the rest of the leads in your database.

Never put all your marketing resources into one or two expensive programs. Marketers who use their budgets on one major effort to attract leads or sales tend to be enamored of their own products and offers, and believe others will be equally interested in hearing all the juicy details. Instead of one-time, high-risk efforts, successful marketers boost their results (and spread their risk) over several smaller campaigns. They know it is usually better to spend a little less on each promotion, but to go to the market with more frequent promotions.

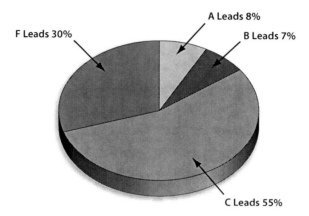

Quality of Leads from B2B Marketing Programs

Start by developing a promotional schedule that allows you to create a lasting, positive image in the minds of your prospects and, equally important, catch them at the precise moment they are in a buying or consideration cycle. Most often, you will need to communicate more, not less, frequently. You may not want to do this because you believe frequent communications offend prospects and make them less likely to buy. This will be true if what you send prospects is a bunch of hard sell and unwanted communications. Then they will definitely lump you in with their other junk mail, spam and disruptive telemarketing calls.

To avoid being portrayed as this type of marketer, start practicing the art of *friendly persistence*. Once you identify a prospect as a legitimate prospect, that person/business should hear from you on as regular a basis as your budget allows. This is particularly important if you have already qualified them as having the money, authority, need, and desire for your products or services.

The key is the *friendly* half of the friendly persistence formula, because it relates to how you make contact with your prospect base. For instance, while you should make compelling offers and market aggressively, you should be careful about practicing hard-sell techniques, particularly early in the sales cycle. While such tactics may win occasional short-term increases in business, they will scuttle your primary mission of building long-term customer relationships.

Another way to keep it friendly is to blend in informational communications with your other promotions, to show your prospects that you are an expert in your industry and enjoy sharing this expertise to help others. Newsletter mailings (print or email) and your blog can also help establish the right climate, so that when you do make contact by phone, or with a sales-oriented promotion, your prospects perceive it as a friendly communication, not as an annoyance or threat.

Here is an example of a recent lead nurturing campaign:

Day 1:	Postcard with white paper offer
Day 4:	Email with same white paper offer
Day 6:	Phone call with same white paper offer and notification of upcoming Web seminar
Day 8:	Postcard regarding Web seminar
Day 12:	Phone call about Web seminar
Day 14:	Email regarding Web seminar
Day 22:	Phone call after the Web seminar offering a link to the recording
Day 24:	Email after the Web seminar offering a link to the recording and the white paper

As you can see, this campaign consisted of eight communications over 24 days, but note that we used no single medium more than three times. Also, the offers were soft (Web seminar and white paper), not a hard sales pitch. This use of friendly persistence helped us achieve a 5.4 percent overall response rate and generated dozens of highly qualified leads.

> **Success Tip:** Use conversion ratios and friendly persistence to create a powerful lead engine to feed your marketing and sales machine.

Chapter 17

Synchronize Marketing and Sales for Superior Performance

"The big money goes to those companies with superior marketing operations. Entrepreneurial companies of today must evolve from being sales oriented to being marketing oriented in order to win the consumer."

— Scott DeGarmo

If you are a marketing manager at a company that uses direct sales representatives, these people can be either your best friends or worst nightmare. Chances are they are somewhere in between, but the point is they can make your life easier, or they can be a constant source of irritation and give you more heartburn than an anchovy pizza at 1 a.m.

Marketing and sales have always had an interdependent relationship. Each department depends on the other for its success, yet they are each quick to point to the other when things are not going well.

Here is an all too common dialogue:

Sales VP –   You aren't giving us enough leads...

Marketing VP –   We gave you plenty of leads, in fact more than enough...

Sales VP –	I'm talking about real leads, not the crap you've been giving us...
Marketing VP –	We spent a lot of money on those leads...
Sales VP –	Then you should ask for a refund because they stink...
Marketing VP –	What stinks is the fact that your salespeople don't know how to close the great leads we are giving them...
Sales VP –	Oh yeah, well, your mother... (you get the drift of where this is heading).

Such a conversation indicates a deadly situation that can end up in a business divorce, where the sales VP and marketing VP are at each other's throats and try to use the CEO as a referee. If you are the marketing executive, you will most likely lose this battle, and you may well find yourself bounced out of the company. Unless you are practicing Fusion Marketing, which means you are a results-driven, revenue-impacting contributor, the CEO will find it easier to sacrifice you to protect his meal ticket (the sales VP). Fair or unfair, it is more often than not the way these things shake out.

Symptoms of a Gap Between Sales and Marketing

While some of the tension between marketing and sales will be obvious, there are several not-so-obvious ways that this can be manifested, including:

- Sales has its own marketing plan

- Sales has its own marketing budget

- Sales people think they can *out-market* the marketing department

- Marketing managers are forced to doctor reports to justify their existence

- Sales routinely blames marketing for its failure to make quota

And the worst sign of all: Sales and marketing won't meet without their attorneys present. Obviously, I'm exaggerating to make a point. But there are many organizations where the leaders of sales and marketing act more like combatants than colleagues. Why is this so, and what can we do about it?

Intentions are usually good—after all, both the marketing and sales departments want not only to achieve their unique objectives, but also to contribute to the overall success of the company. Yet despite these good intentions, many initiatives fail due to a lack of cooperation between the marketing and sales departments.

The easiest course of action is to simply design and implement the system that works best for the marketing department. In the short term, this will save you many hours of frustration, but you may be setting up your marketing program for certain long-term failure. Your counterparts in the sales organizations have many ways to frustrate your best efforts, so it is best to acknowledge this fact and create the right foundation for joint success.

How to Build a Good Working Relationship with Sales

The following steps are essential in establishing a productive working relationship between marketing and sales departments:

1. As a marketing manager, you must take full responsibility for the success or failure of the program. Although

sales is an integral part of the process, lead generation is rightfully considered a marketing function.

2. Sales managers, and also sales reps, should be brought into the design phase of the program. They must feel that their input receives full consideration and they must buy into the program before it is implemented.

3. Salespeople should feel that the system rewards them for cooperation. The best reward is for them to be able to make more sales with no extra effort. Show them how the system rewards them for working smarter, not harder. Never institute a new system at the same time you take any negative action (such as cutting sales territories), or you will permanently link the two events in the minds of the sales department. You must keep everything positive.

4. Feedback loops should be put in place. Sales reps must always be kept abreast of changes and upgrades in the end-to-end process. Likewise, you should regularly solicit their input on how the process is working.

5. You must get agreement on the technical aspects of the lead-to-sales system. The ideal structure will combine a great deal of flexibility for field sales reps with maximum control by the marketing department (not the other way around), and ensure that relevant information about all prospects will be captured. You must always remember that all prospect and customer data belongs to the company, and not to the individual sales rep.

6. Sales and marketing must agree on what constitutes

a good lead, because this definition will drive much of the marketing department's efforts. The criteria for what constitutes a hot lead or qualified lead forms part of the basis for a service level agreement (SLA) between the marketing and sales departments.

How to Quantify the Marketing Contribution

One way to create a mutually respectful and appreciative relationship is to have a written understanding of what the sales department expects and what it will require to make its revenue targets. Always start with the revenue numbers and work backward. However, do not just take the entire revenue number and assume that you need to supply all the inquiries, leads, and qualified leads that are necessary to hit that target.

For example, an established company with a quarterly revenue target of $10 million may find that fifty percent of more of this number is run-rate business that will come in regardless of what marketing does. Cross-sales, add-on sales, maintenance sales, and some channel revenues are examples of this type of run-rate business. I have seen situations where marketing's contribution to revenue is as little as ten percent and as high as ninety percent. Regardless, this is the number you should focus on.

For an example of how this works, let us assume that your organization utilizes a direct sales force (either field sales or telephone) to close business. And let's continue to use the $10 million figure as the quarterly revenue quota. You (the marketing VP) and the sales VP agree that forty percent of this number is influenced by marketing. Again, working backward, you work out some targets for every step of the process:

Average deal size: $50,000

Number of new deals needed to reach revenue goal:
$4,000,000/$50,000 = 80 deals

Closure rate of opportunities to closed deals: 1 out of 5

Number of opportunities needed to create deals: 80 × 5 = 400

Ratio of opportunities to qualified leads: 1 out of 4

Number of qualified leads needed: 4 × 400 = 1,600

Ratio of qualified leads to raw leads (inquiries): 1 out of 12

Number of raw leads/inquiries needed: 12 × 1,600 = 19,200

Once you and your sales counterpart have established each of these crucial metrics, you then come to agreement as to who is responsible for which part of the process. In this scenario, the marketing VP is most likely responsible for every step through qualified leads, and the sales VP is responsible for opportunities and revenue. Therefore, if the hand-off from marketing to sales is at the qualified lead stage, then you must gain agreement as to what exactly constitutes a qualified lead. This negotiation is critical for both parties because it will be used as a basis for evaluating future performance. Be careful of overpromising, because it is better to under-promise and over-deliver than vice versa.

As I discussed in the chapter on building a lead engine, a qualified lead is defined as one that comes from a company with:

- An identified project

- A budget for that project

- A specific time frame for purchase (e.g., one to three months or four to six months)

- An identified decision-maker

Once the ratios are determined and definitions established for each phase of the process, the result is a service level agreement (SLA) that establishes a covenant between the marketing and sales groups. The marketing executive promises to deliver a certain quantity of raw leads, qualified leads, or whatever the sales department works with, and the sales executive promises to work their part of the process diligently to ensure that the hard work of the marketing department is rewarded with results that really matter—new customers and fresh revenue.

In addition to the ratios listed above, make sure your SLA includes details on:

- Number of leads required and when

- What constitutes a *sales ready* lead

- How leads are distributed to the field

- How sales reps disposition leads

- How marketing's contribution is measured through a closed-loop system

A closed-loop marketing and sales system consists of two primary parts. The first, represented by the graphic below, outlines the process by which inbound inquiries are managed. Sources of incoming inquiries are listed on the left side of the diagram. These inquiries are put through a filtering process that can either be Web-based (asking questions on a Web form) or telephone-based (asking questions via phone). Qualified leads are then routed to the appropriate sales channel for immediate follow-up. Inquires with future potential are added to the database for remarketing efforts. Unqualified leads, including competitors, are put into the suppression file, and will be excluded from future marketing campaigns.

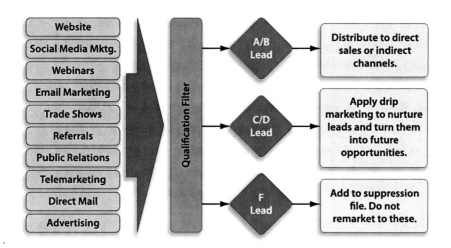

Lead Qualification Process

The second component of the closed-loop system is a method to measure the end-to-end metrics of the marketing and sales process and quantify the sources of your revenue. Ideally, this data will come out of a customer relationship management (CRM) system. If you cannot produce the data in an automated fashion, you can use an interactive Web process or correlate your new sales orders to the prospect database. If all these methods are unrealistic, then interview the sales reps who sold the deals or conduct customer "why did you buy?" surveys. Regardless of how you produce the data, you must have it to effectively match marketing expenditures to revenue.

> *Success Tip:* Synchronizing the marketing and sales functions can help create great success, especially when a service level agreement outlines the duties and objectives of each department.

Chapter 18

Create an Unstoppable Sales Machine

"There are worse things in life than death. Have you ever spent an evening with an insurance salesman?"

–Woody Allen

Most of this book has been focused on marketing. But if you have a role in the sales process, you will find this chapter particularly important. Even if you stay strictly on the marketing side of the fence, it is a good idea to understand what your colleagues in sales are experiencing. In B2B marketing, sales is usually your most important customer, and if they fail, you fail. The goal (necessity) is to have a well-oiled end-to-end marketing and sales machine that will accomplish the corporate objectives. To do this, practice the first key to creating an unstoppable sales machine: **Make sure there is complete alignment between the marketing and sales departments**. A service level agreement (as discussed in the previous chapter) will help keep the alignment on track.

Even though I find the quote at the top of this page amusing, I don't agree with it. One of my closest friends is an insurance salesman and he never talks business at our parties. Nonetheless, the quote illustrates the negative context people have of salespeople in general. The perception is that salespeople will do anything to sell you stuff you don't really need. This brings me to the second key: **Concentrate your efforts on finding the companies and individuals that have a genuine need for what you offer**. Isn't this a much easier and less stressful way of doing things, for you and your prospects? Response rates will be higher, close rates will be higher, and you will not have to manipulate anyone.

The next key is one that truly separates the world-class sales organizations from the also-rans: **Never lose a deal alone**. Selling at its best is a team effort and it is a serious error to lose a possible deal because the sales rep neglected to bring in the rest of his or her teammates. You need to be very aggressive about letting your reps know about all the resources they have available to help them at every stage of the sales process. And one of the most important resources you can provide is a fresh perspective.

A good way to kill the productivity of a sales force is to throw too much at them. Too many products, too many offers, and too many messages equate to too many chances for the sales team to mess things up and lose sales. One of my clients had great technology, but had a very bad habit of changing its product offerings and value proposition every six months or so. The sales team was encouraged to spend their time on the newest offerings instead of what had worked for them in the past. This required extensive retraining of the team, and they never found their rhythm. To avoid this problem, my next important sales key is: **Keep things simple and focused on as few priorities as possible**.

One thing that offends me greatly is to see sales departments mishandle the leads/inquiries given to them by the marketing department. I have seen sales reps ignore leads, denigrate leads, and follow them up in a half-hearted manner. Often this occurs because the VP of Sales speaks poorly about what marketing is doing, creating a culture where reps feel it is okay not to work the leads they are given. This is a terrible waste of resources, and if your company is allowing this to happen, I encourage you to immediately stop the practice. Leads cost money and few of us have extra money to flush down the toilet. If the lead quality is not where it needs to be, re-read the chapter on creating a service level agreement (SLA) between marketing and sales, and practice the recommendations. And always practice this most important key to effective sales: **Treat sales leads with care and respect.**

My next key to creating an unstoppable sales machine is: **Be different, be unique, be provocative.** Have you seen the bumper sticker that says *Why Be Normal* (with Normal spelled upside down)? This is a good posture to take when it comes to selling. If you have the same pitch as everyone else in your industry, delivered in the same way, you are bound to get the same result: mediocrity. Geoffrey Moore, who taught a generation of marketers with his books *Crossing the Chasm* and *Inside the Tornado*, now teaches a methodology called Provocation Selling. Instead of playing nice, you should poke where it hurts, challenge the prevailing view, and address the unacknowledged critical issues. This will get you past the typical limitations of budget, sales cycle, access to the decision-maker, and so forth.

Another important key is: **Have a highly flexible sales process.** While *flexible process* may sound like an oxymoron, sales is both an art and a science. If you over-engineer the process, you can end up with a group of sales reps that will do anything you tell them, except the most important thing—close business. Sales is a game of technique but also one of instinct and intuition. Thinking and acting outside of the box is okay as long as it falls within reasonable limits.

Many sales managers are good at telling their people what to do, but not so good at supporting them. But the more you try to direct someone's actions, the more the ownership is retained by you, instead of by the rep, where it belongs. The key here is to **create a culture of accountability and support**. The sales rep's job is to produce his or her revenue targets. Your job is not to tell your staff how to make their numbers; it is to support them in every way in achieving their goals.

To summarize, here are the Eight Keys to creating an unstoppable sales machine:

1. Make sure there is complete alignment between the marketing and sales departments.

2. Concentrate your efforts on finding the companies and individuals that have a genuine need for what you offer.

3. Never lose a deal alone.

4. Keep things simple and focused on as few priorities as possible.

5. Treat sales leads with care and respect.

6. Be different, be unique, be provocative.

7. Have a highly flexible sales process.

8. Create a culture of accountability and support.

Success Tip: Practice the Eight Keys to create an unstoppable sales machine and your results will soar.

Chapter 19

Construct a Great Channel Program

"If you make a product good enough, even though you live in the depths of the forest, the public will make a path to your door, says the philosopher. But if you want the public in sufficient numbers, you better construct a highway."

– William Randolph Hearst

If you decide to go with either a pure or a hybrid channel sales model, make sure that you create the best foundation for success. You don't have to do everything yourself. Channel recruitment and management are highly specialized and there are companies that can handle parts of this process including channel program setup, reseller recruitment, vertical strategies, coverage models, creation of incentive and loyalty programs, lead generation, training, and support.

If you decide to find your own channel partners, here are some good sources:

- Your competitors – This is an excellent source because the partners who currently do business with your competitors are already familiar with the industry and the types of products and services that you offer. Target your competitors' resellers with pricing, margin, marketing, and training incentives.

- Industry conferences and events – Willie Sutton said that he robbed banks because "that's where the money is." Likewise, you should go to industry events because that is where you can find potential partners. Many will not be looking for a new product or service line to handle, but a few will. You need to nurture these relationships over time, so be patient and make sure you keep prospective partners in your email and social media communications loop.

- The Internet – Make sure your Website displays a clear vision of the benefits of doing business with your firm, as well as the process that a new partner will need to follow in order to do business with you.

- Referrals from your existing partners – Partners will be happy to refer other companies to you as long as they are non-competitive in their specific market area.

Perhaps the best source of new partners is the character and integrity that you practice as a channel-friendly organization. Partners know the good guys to do business with, and you want to be perceived as one of the good guys. Here are five ideas on how to co-market with your partners:

1. Have a published co-op marketing program.

2. Always make your partner put skin in the game.

3. Don't waste leads on partners that don't aggressively follow up.

4. Always maintain control of the leads you give to partners.

5. Manage leads as part of each partner's business plan.

If you choose to offer co-marketing programs, make sure you have the proper metrics in place to measure items such as sales volume, growth rate, product share, history of making quota, lead closure rate, and customer satisfaction.

If your product is not currently channel-friendly, you will need to make it more attractive to your partners and their customers. Start by looking at ways to standardize and reduce the number of model choices. Likewise, simplify products by reducing the number of features, and use every method you can think of to streamline the buying process.

How to Manage Channel Conflict

Companies run away from the potential of channel conflict as if it were the plague. They cite issues such as the fact that channel conflict can kill deals, leads to friction with your direct sales team, causes the channel to leave you for your competitor, and leads you to make ill-informed business decisions. These are the negative aspects of working with a channel that you will have to take into account.

However, if managed properly, channel conflict can be a good thing. At first blush, this statement may seem counterintuitive. After all, who wants a bunch of channel partners who are fighting over deals with each other or with your direct sales reps? However, a little conflict can be healthy and cause everyone to work harder and give you the security necessary to terminate under-performing reps/partners. Conversely, a lack of conflict can mean a lack of strong deal flow. Likewise, the absence of conflict often means that nobody cares (a very bad sign), while managed conflict can create competition that benefits all parts of your business.

If your partners are not pursuing deals aggressively, they are not making you money. And if you have several partners in a particular geography and they aren't bumping in to each other, it indicates that you have anemic coverage in that area. There are ways to manage the conflict, for example, by tightly defining who gets which type of lead (by industry, size, geography, solution type, etc.). But my basic philosophy has been, in cases of conflict, always err on the side of whoever has the best chance of bringing in the business.

Seven Lessons for Working with a Channel

Some companies perceive that adopting a channel strategy will solve many of the problems that have prevented them from achieving their revenue or profit objectives. After all, it is a compelling proposition to have external companies working for your success without the heavy investments necessary to build, equip, and train an internal sales organization—particularly if that organization is geographically scattered. However, there are some tough lessons I have learned over many channel relationships, some painful, some amusing, and some highly productive.

Lesson 1 – The channel partners are in it for themselves. Regardless of how many times you hear adages from your partners such as, "Consider us an extension of your sales force" or "We're all in this together," remember that when the going gets tough, the partner will make decisions in its own best interest. The channel will often prove harder to manage than your employees will because you do not have the power of the regular paycheck to control their behavior. In fact, your partners have their own sets of problems and their own payrolls to meet, and they will support you and your ideas only to the extent that you contribute to their monetary success.

Lesson 2 – You must create win-win scenarios. Since the partners' primary motivation is the success of their own businesses and the feeding of their own families, why would you expect them to cooperate in a program that was not in their best interests? I have seen companies create greed-driven scenarios—such as offering ridiculously low margins, or charging outrageous registration fees—in order to generate short-term revenue or higher profit margins for themselves. Quality partners have many options, so why would they accept anything other than reasonable entry fees and revenue splits? Do yourself a favor and design a program that will attract, instead of repel, desirable channel partners.

Lesson 3 – Quality is better than quantity. The Pareto Principle definitely applies to channel partners, since you will often get eighty to ninety percent of your revenue from a small fraction of your partners. Too often, the primary focus is on partner acquisition. Regional reps (and their managers) get excited when they sign up new partners, figuring that every new partner is a steady source of future revenue. However, the fact is, a small minority of channel partners will usually account for the vast majority of your deal flow so it is better to focus on fewer numbers of quality partners. To put this another way, I would rather have ten active and engaged partners instead of thirty who have signed the agreement but are not committed to the partnership.

Lesson 4 – The best partners are the ones who bring you business, with minimal effort on your part. You are probably ready to say "duh" as you read this lesson, but let me explain. There are those partners who require lots of time and attention from you and cannot seem to close business on their own. They want you to bring them prospects and then require you to help them close the deal. Considering that you are giving up a bunch of your revenue when a partner closes the deal (otherwise known as *margin*), why does it make sense for you to go out of your way to feed such partners with fresh leads? A better strategy is to find channel partners who have access to their own leads and prospects and who can bring you that magical substance known as *incremental revenue*. Once partners prove that they can sell their own leads and prospects, especially in a self-sufficient manner, then by all means share some of your leads with those partners.

Lesson 5 – Selling is easier than sustaining. There are many steps necessary to get new partners productive, and if you do not follow these steps, many new and promising partnerships will wither on the vine. Some organizations have solved this problem by supplementing their partner sales reps with partner enablement specialists. The job of the enablement specialist is to work closely with each new partner to do whatever it takes to bring in the first few deals. Once this happens, the partnership is more likely to bear fruit far into the future.

Lesson 6 – Training is everything. With few exceptions, the companies that provide their channel partners with the greatest quantity and quality of training have the most successful partner programs. This is true for two primary reasons. First, the better they know the specifics of your offering and how to sell it, the more effective they will be at generating initial deals. The lack of initial deals increases the likelihood of not getting future deals from that partner. Reason two is that a partner that commits its team to a training program is putting serious skin in the game. A sales rep who sits through days of your training is not generating revenue, and this is a real investment on the part of the partner, who will want to see that investment rewarded with future revenue.

Lesson 7 – Say YES to your partners. Organizations spend enormous amounts of time and money putting together voluminous partner plans or partner handbooks, detailing every possible aspect of the relationship. Unfortunately, they then use the plan/handbook to say NO to partner requests, and justify this by claiming that the same rules apply to every partner, and no exceptions can be made. This is one of those examples demonstrated by Doug Bader's expression, "Rules are for the guidance of wise men and the obedience of fools." If you do not want to be a fool, figure out a way to help your partners with their particular marketing and other needs. Of course, you need to practice judgment— you do not want to invest major resources in something that has only a minor upside, but there are many ways you can help partners in a cost-effective way. This will gain you the reputation as a good company to do business with, and this reputation will attract great new partners to you.

Success *Tip:* Find good partners and practice the lessons for working with a channel.

Part V

Choosing Your Best Marketing Media and Tactics

Chapter 20

Design a Strategic Website

"The power of a Website comes from the people using it, not the people making it."

–Chris Edwards

When it comes to Website design, form should always follow function. Many organizations come up with a nice design and then fit in all the components. However, you should not involve a graphic designer until you figure out exactly what you want your Website to accomplish. There are many possible design templates and your choice will depend on the specific objectives for the site. For example, the primary purpose of your Website could be:

- Creating awareness.

- Conveying information (education).

- Establishing expertise.

- Generating leads.

- Selling a product or service (taking orders).

- Raising funds.

- Advocating for a cause.

You get the picture. Websites are no longer just online brochures. They command action. And the type of action you want the prospect or existing customer to take must be represented in the construction of your site. Think of this in terms of an active process—how specific types of people will find what they are looking for and interact with you—not in terms of a static site with a bunch of information tabs (About Us, Products, Services, News, etc.), but rather in terms of how prospects will be guided along the path that leads to their becoming customers.

Once you have decided the overall purpose of the Website, you should establish specific goals for the site. Examples include:

1. Percentage of growth in visitor traffic.

2. Stickiness of the site in terms of amount of time per visit and number of pages viewed.

3. Numbers of inquiries/leads generated via Web forms.

4. Amount of traffic generated by organic search terms.

5. Amount of traffic generated by third party Website referrals.

6. Performance of specific offers.

7. Google PageRank.

The last measurement, PageRank, is a vital indicator of how important a Website is in the eyes of Google (these are very significant eyes). Google looks at all links to your site and interprets such links as *votes* to your site's worthiness. Votes from sites that are themselves important count more than votes from non-important sites. Google also looks at factors such as numbers of visitors and prevalence of search terms on the page. While PageRank is not the only thing to measure, it is a good overall indicator of the stickiness of your site and how it compares to your competitors. Depending on where you are starting from, you may want to aim for a PageRank of 5-8 (on a scale of 0-10).

Depending on the strength of your existing Website, you may be able to modify it to get the results you want or you may have to recreate it on a new platform. For example, there are Websites built on older architectures or HTML that have little chance of rising in PageRank or search engine optimization. These sites will never be *sticky* and you will pay a large price in terms of the number of visitors in order to maintain the current site infrastructure.

The good news is that new open source technology allows you to have a sophisticated and optimized Website at much lower cost. Two excellent open source products are Joomla and Drupal. If your requirements are modest, you can create a decent Website using a tool such as WordPress – which provides not only a free blogging site at wordpress.com, but also a Website content management publishing platform at www.wordpress.org.

Tips for Creating a Strategic Website

Whether you choose to revamp an existing Website or build a new one, make sure you include these design and content factors:

1. Design it for your key constituencies – The fact that your board and executives like the Website is a good thing, but not the most important factor. Remember who you are designing the site for—your prospects, customers, partners, and so forth. Make sure you understand what they will be looking for and provide it to them.

2. Start with a *Content Map* – Like a site map, a content map contains a listing of every page of your Website but you organize it in terms of the information provided on

specific pages. A content map will provide a visual representation of the navigation path to every bit of content on the Website.

3. Keep the message simple and clear – Avoid the tendency to cram your entire story into as little space as possible (which creates a cluttered site and makes information much harder to find). Frustrated Web surfers do not tend to become customers, so "hiding the information" is a game you should not play.

4. Layer the content – Rather than having pages that run on endlessly, and require a lot of scrolling, break up the content. Start with short descriptions (paragraph size) on the home page (level one content), link to single page copy on the same subject (level two content), and from there, you can include more in-depth and lengthy descriptive copy (levels three and four content). This will make your text easier to read and create a richer looking Website.

5. Simple navigation – Create your tabs, categories, etc., to be intuitive, and thus, easy to follow. Watch the use of industry jargon and company-specific names. Provide links to different parts of the site to prevent visitors from becoming stuck. The point is to allow prospects to quickly find exactly what they are looking for.

6. Optimize for organic search – This is extremely important because it is a low-cost way of driving traffic. Search engine optimization (SEO) will also benefit your pay per click (PPC) efforts by giving you better quality scores. More about SEO and PPC in the next chapter.

7. Think *sticky* – Make sure your prospects find plenty of value on your Website so they keep coming back. Remember that value isn't just the benefits of your products and services, but also (and more important to the prospect), information that will help them do their jobs better.

8. Think *dynamic* – Websites get out-of-date quickly if the content is static. By changing content on a regular basis, you give visitors a reason to become repeat visitors and customers. The home page is most important, but don't let entire sections of the site go stale.

9. Offers, offers, offers – Make sure you give visitors plenty of opportunities to interact with you. Virtually every page on your site should contain an offer. If the information you are providing has significant value, trade that information for data about the prospect and for his or her permission to allow you to communicate with them in the future. You will reap major benefits from this permission-based database building approach.

10. Incorporate social media – If you have the time to do it right, a blog can be a terrific way to create Website stickiness. Read the chapter on social media for more information on how to start and maintain a blog.

11. Borrow good ideas – One of the great things about the World Wide Web is the transparency. You can see how every one of your competitors, and every other company, builds its site and portrays its message. You can see the information they provide, their offers, and what they say on their blog. Just make sure you are borrowing, not *stealing*.

12. Provide relevant information – Remember that many prospects like to do their investigation via the Internet before interacting with companies. They are looking for reasons to label you as a potential supplier or to cross you off the list. You may be tempted to withhold information for fear that competitors will learn your secrets, but you are usually better off providing more, not less, information.

13. Measure your Website effectiveness – If you are going to use your Website as an important part of your marketing and sales program, make sure you carefully measure performance of this critical asset.

Measuring Website Effectiveness

We talked above about the importance of setting measurable objectives for your Website. So how do you benchmark performance against your objectives? The simplest (and free) tool to use is Google Analytics. However, this gives you only a partial picture. I prefer one of the inexpensive Web-based services like Web CEO ($199 per year at webceo.com) or VisiStat ($249 per year at visistat.com). You can find many other solutions (including user reviews) at CNET Downloads (download.cnet.com). Simply type "Web analytics" in the query box at the top of the page. A tool for measuring your monthly traffic against competitors is available at siteanalytics.compete.com.

Another excellent (and free) Website analytics tool is Website Grader from HubSpot (grader.com). By simply providing your Website address, you will get tons of useful information including Google PageRank, page analysis, number of external links, blog ranking, and much more. You can list your chief competitors and see how they compare. The site also gives you an overall marketing effectiveness score. For example, at one of my large B2B clients, the Website scores at ninety-six percent on the effectiveness scale, versus eighty-eight percent and eighty percent for its largest competitors—giving the company a significant Web marketing advantage. You should shoot for similar advantages against your rivals.

Following is an example of the analytics I collect for business-to-business Websites. All of this data is delivered in a dashboard view. I break it down between macro reports, which show the overall health of the Website, and micro reports, which show the performance of individual parts of the Website:

Macro Data Reports

1.   Total of all visitors to Website

2.   Total unique visitors to Website

3.   Total page views on Website

4.   Average page views per visitor

5.   Average time duration per visit

6.   Google PageRank

7.   Website Grader marketing efficiency

Micro Data Reports

1.   Best performing referring URLs

2.   Best performing organic and paid search keywords (by number of visitors)

3.   Click-through rate for organic and paid search keywords

4. Cost per lead and conversion rate of paid search terms

5. Pages visited most often

6. Primary click paths (entry and exit)

7. Bounce rate (abandonment) for each page

8. Conversion rate of landing page and offers

This may seem like a lot of information to maintain, but it is much simpler once you have the tool to capture and organize the data into a dashboard view.

Success *Tip:* Build your Website for prospects and customers, not your executives or board members.

Chapter 21

Drive Leads with Pay Per Click and Search Optimization

"It is not the job of search engine optimization to make a pig fly. It is the job of the SEO to genetically reengineer the Website so that it becomes an eagle."

— Lisa Barone

Throughout this book, I have suggested that you build a strong online presence. The previous chapter listed some techniques for creating a compelling and useful Website. Now we are going to take your online marketing to the next level with pay per click (PPC) and search engine optimization (SEO).

Depending on the size of your organization and budget, it may be better to outsource these online acceleration tactics, or to hire an expert to join your staff. You can't be good at everything, and PPC and SEO are very specialized techniques. However, learning at least the basics of PPC and SEO can help you evaluate the performance of your contractors and internal staff. There are a lot of mediocre PPC and SEO performers out there, so be very careful about whom you choose to assist you.

Pay per click is defined by Wikipedia as "an Internet advertising model used on search engines, advertising networks, and content sites, such as blogs, in which advertisers pay their host only when their ad is clicked. Websites that utilize PPC ads display an advertisement when a keyword query matches an advertiser's keyword list, or when a content site displays relevant content. Such advertisements are called *sponsored links* or *sponsored ads*, and appear adjacent to or above organic results on search engine results pages, or anywhere a web developer chooses on a content site."

Wikipedia defines search engine optimization as "the process of improving the volume or quality of traffic to a Website from search engines via 'natural' ('organic' or 'algorithmic') search results. Typically, the earlier a site appears in the search results list, the more visitors it will receive from the search engine. As an Internet marketing strategy, SEO considers what people are searching for and how search engines work. Optimizing a Website primarily involves editing its content and HTML coding to both increase its relevance to specific keywords and to remove barriers to the indexing activities of search engines."

Pay per click and search engine optimization have many similarities but they have one big difference. You pay a fee for everyone who finds you through PPC while you pay nothing for visitors who find you through an organic search term (aside from the monthly optimization fee, if you use an outside expert). This is why you must build your Website on a platform that is optimized for search and why you should use SEO techniques to make your Website *search engine friendly*. The good news is that not only is SEO an extremely cost-effective way of driving traffic to your Website—success in organic search optimization has a direct impact on the cost-effectiveness of your PPC program.

There are many PPC providers, but the big three are Google Ad-Words, Yahoo! Search Marketing, and Microsoft adCenter. I suggest that you start with Google because it is by far the largest and has many built-in tools to help you get started. There are a lot of moving parts to PPC marketing so it's an excellent idea for you to read a good book on the subject. I highly recommend the *Ultimate Guide to Google AdWords* by Perry Marshall and Bryan Todd.

Strategies for Pay Per Click Success

The PPC process begins with someone entering a search term into his or her computer. They are then presented with a list of paid text ads that Google or other providers serve up, based on the relevance of the term and the amount bid by particular companies to buy that keyword. The person can choose to click on one or more ads or leave the search page. If they do click on your ad, they will be taken to your Website, offer landing-page, or wherever you direct them.

It is important for you to make sure the search term, ad, and landing page relate closely in terms of copy, offer, and so forth. For example, if your search term is something like "low cost Web design", you would not use an ad that talked about how creative your designs were and your landing page would not have an offer related to Web design techniques. You need to align the messaging all the way through the process—in this case by appealing to the economic buyer. You may have another set of keywords relating to the strength of your design skills, with matching ads and landing pages. The PPC process is highly targeted and the more specific you make it for specific types of prospects, the more success you will have.

Here are some more tips to help get your PPC efforts off to a good start:

- Start slowly – Just as you wouldn't dump a lot of money into the stock market without doing your homework, don't make the mistake of spending your entire budget before you understand what you are doing.

- Test everything – PPC is like a high-performance sports car. You must constantly tune the program to get the best results and that means lots of testing. Test keywords, ads, landing pages, headlines, and offers.

- Put your keywords (search terms) in your ad copy – Google will reward you with a better quality score and you will often get a better page position at lower cost.

- Target carefully – Create personas of your potential prospects and create keywords, ads, and landing pages for these specific individuals.

- Do not go for the top page position – Your best value for the cost vs. page position is three to five spots from the top of the page.

- Take your prospects to a landing page that contains an offer, not to the home page of your Website. You need to capture their information so that you can begin your follow-up and remarketing efforts.

- Use PPC to test the search terms, ad copy, and offers. You can do this very quickly and use what you learn to adjust your Website copy and search engine optimization strategy.

There are four primary measurements you should use to track the performance of your pay per click campaigns:

1. Click through rate (CTR): the number of people who click on your ad divided by the total number of impressions. Many companies settle for about one percent, but you should aim for two to three percent.

2. Cost per click (CPC): how much it costs you to get someone to click on your ad. This is highly dependent on the type of product or service you are selling and the competition for the keywords.

3. Conversion rate: how many people fill out your Web form after going to your landing page. Conversion rates range from two to three percent to as much as ten percent. I have had great success with PPC programs that deliver five to seven percent conversions.

4. Cost per conversion (CPC): how much it costs you to get someone to fill out your Web form. All of the other metrics influence this one. CPC costs can range from a few dollars to a hundred dollars or more depending on the competition and selling price of the keyword.

Strategies for Search Engine Optimization Success

It is tough out there in cyberspace. Your Website has to compete with many others for attention. So how do you ensure that the right people find their way to your site? One of the most effective, and least costly, is to optimize your Website to take advantage of search terms. For example, if you are a provider of accounting services in Santa Fe, New Mexico, and someone types "Santa Fe accounting" in their search window, you want to be among the first few entries when the search results appear. If you are buried at the bottom of page one, or even worse, on page two or later, that prospect will never know you existed.

To find out where you stand, put yourself in the shoes of someone who is researching the type of product or service you provide and start typing in search terms to find your PageRank. There are automated tools to help you find your search rank for specific terms but the point really hits home when you type in the terms one by one. This is especially true when your competitor is high on page one and you are nowhere to be found. To make sure you don't miss any important keywords, use one of the free tools such as the Google Adwords Keyword Tool or WordTracker to determine what keywords people search on in a particular category.

As mentioned in the chapter on building your Website, you should take advantage of HubSpot's terrific (and free) Website analysis tool at website. grader.com. This tells you where you stand in terms of the marketing effectiveness of your Website and gives you many details on issues such as Google PageRank, number of links to your site, text readability, and much more. This is an indication as to the relative strength of your Website.

If you score low on visibility, this may be due to limitations in your Website architecture or design. If so, either correct those deficiencies or if necessary, rebuild the site in a manner that makes things easy to find for search engine robots (also known as spiders or crawlers). These robots travel throughout the Web to collect information on the text contained at each Website. They first look at things like titles and meta tags, and then move on to body text. A lot of the stuff that makes your Website cool, such as Flash, frames, JavaScript, drop-down lists, etc., actually impedes the robot's search. Robots like simple architectures and they are partial to text links. In addition, they much prefer static pages to dynamically built pages.

Just as with pay per click, there is a lot involved in search engine optimization, and some of it is technical, so you should read a book or two on the subject. Here are some additional ideas on how to get a better position in the search engine rankings.

- Focus on content. Even great SEO tips will not help you if your content is poor or not relevant to your target audience.

- Add new content on a regular basis. Search engines don't like stale sites and for that matter, neither do prospects.

- Social media helps your Website's visibility enormously.

- Start a blog. In addition to all the other good reasons to start a blog, it also helps your site to become more visible. Search engines love blogs because they are constantly being replenished with fresh content.

- Include a site map. The site map makes it much easier for the robots to find all the information on your Website.

- Create a relevant title name and meta description for each page of your Website. Use the desired search term in the title name. This really helps your rankings.

- Have many links to your Website and make sure that some of these links go to content within the site, not just to the home page. This way, your site is assigned a higher value because it appears to be content-rich.

- Be generous with linking to other high-quality Websites. This will increase the likelihood of them linking to you. If you use image links in your navigation bar, also include text links, and put the text links before the image links. Otherwise, the robots will ignore them.

- Do not overstuff your pages with keywords. Search engines prefer natural language text and if the keywords appear too often, this counts against you.

- Think of repurposing the content you have on the Website. For example, are there white papers that you can turn into Web pages, or press releases that can take on the look of blog postings?

- Analyze the original keyword choices every six months. Searchers key in new keywords, and some current terms fall out of favor.

Success Tip: Learn the basics of pay per click and search engine optimization even if you pay an outside contractor for these services.

Chapter 22

Leverage Social Media to Expand Your Influence

"If I wouldn't say it to a reporter, I wouldn't say it on my blog."

–Jason Goldberg

Social media encompasses many of the new interactive formats including blogging, Twitter, Facebook, MySpace, Internet forums, YouTube, podcasts, Google and Yahoo groups, social networks, PeopleBrowsr, Wikipedia and LinkedIn. And this is just a partial list. Although all these vehicles have their purpose, the tools I use most often in the B2B world are blogging, LinkedIn and Twitter. All three tools have been useful for generating awareness, leads and revenue.

The phenomenon of social media has evolved to the point where it has become mainstream. Businesses have increasingly turned their attention and resources toward interactive media because they find it to be an economical and efficient way to get the word out about their companies, products, and services. Despite unclear standards for measuring return on investment, there is a lot of anecdotal evidence for the success of social media, and new companies are joining the bandwagon daily. There are companies which have dropped all traditional marketing media in favor of social media. One example is CodeBaby, a Colorado company that creates Web digital characters for companies that want to improve their customer and prospect experience. You can check out this very interesting concept at www.codebaby.com.

All forms of social media are based on two important attributes, *content* and *interactivity*. Content is created wherever and whenever someone has something useful to say. The definition of *useful* is totally in the mind of the content creator, which means that content has become democratized. Everyone can be a content publisher, regardless if the audience is one (themselves) or millions. This content can be published in many different media and consumed by anyone who has access to the content publishing service. Interactivity occurs because content consumers can add to the content, rate it, comment on it, or distribute it to others.

Examples of what you can accomplish by combining relevant content and social media are endless. David Meerman Scott's book titled *World Wide Rave* talks about how the power of social media can create massive publicity and interest in your product or service, very quickly. The book can show you how to create far more buzz than you thought possible. While few of us are lucky enough (or prepared enough) to find the right timing, circumstances, and techniques to create a true World Wide Rave, we can certainly use the strategies to benefit our organizations.

Creating Your Blog

In the book *Naked Conversations,* Shel Israel and Robert Scoble observed, "In our vision, blogging changes marketing more than marketing changes blogging." Many companies and individuals have found this to be true and have achieved spectacular marketing success with blogging. Because it is a straightforward process and easy to manage, a blog is a good place to delve into social media.

The important first question to ask is whether your social media efforts will be built around your company and brand, or focused on an individual. While personal blogs can be extremely effective at driving the company message, you run the risk of the individual leaving your company and taking the blog audience to their next endeavor. You can mitigate this risk and increase exposure by using multiple bloggers from the organization. If you like, you can have one or more primary bloggers and several secondary or occasional bloggers.

Do not expect instant results from your blogging program. Unless your message is particularly timely and compelling, it takes some time to build an audience. You can supplement your efforts with paid media buys. Always include your blog address as part of your email signature, as well as a link to and from your Website. You can pick up a number of visitors this way.

Before you start your blog, remember that curiosity is an important trait for a blogger. You should learn everything you can about your potential readers. Find out what they care most about and what they need to do their jobs better. Discover their desires, interests, and what they want most from their jobs and personal lives. Then write about these things.

Here are some rules to help you create a compelling and successful blog:

1. Be unique. Do not waste your time rehashing the same content that people can get elsewhere. Readers want a current and fresh look at your topic. Give it to them.

2. Be relevant. Stick to your chosen topic area. People read a marketing blog to learn about marketing and a finance blog to learn about finance. Keep the extraneous text to a minimum.

3. Be interactive. Blogs that generate outside comments tend to be a lot more interesting. Without outside participation, blogs are just another online newsletter.

4. Link back to your corporate Website – but do not overdo the company connection. Over-selling is a quick way to chase away readers.

5. Incorporate search engine research. Use the keywords that people search in your blog title and text, and perhaps create categories with these terms. This will help more people find your blog.

6. Use category tags on your blog. It will help people find you and drive up your search engine rankings.

7. Aggressively share the news about your blog with the outside world. Send everyone on your database a link to the blog.

8. Post new content regularly to keep the blog from getting stale. Every other week is a minimum schedule; post more often if you can.

9. Approve and answer comments as soon as possible. I also suggest that you moderate comments to keep out the spam and sales pitches.

10. Unfortunately, many comments will be almost incoherent, so you should edit these before you allow them to be posted.

A good resource to learn about the world of blogging is copyblogger, found at copyblogger.com. Sonia Simone, copyblogger's senior editor, has published a great deal of useful information about blogging and is herself a first-class blogger.

Using LinkedIn

LinkedIn (linkedin.com) is a terrific social media tool for those who market to businesses. Wiki Answers claims there are 35 million LinkedIn users, and unlike some of the more consumer-oriented tools such as Facebook and MySpace, the vast majority of people use it for business purposes. It is very easy to get started on LinkedIn and you can grow your presence incrementally. Keep in mind that LinkedIn is a relationship medium, not a transaction medium, and you will receive negative feedback if you are too blatant with promoting your business. You can let people know what you do, but subtlety works better than a hard-sell approach.

Here are some tips to make your LinkedIn experience fruitful:

1. Get started by posting your complete profile, including education and past positions. This allows more people to find you and requests to be connected. I have over 400 connections and add one or more almost every week. Many LinkedIn members have thousands of connections. You can choose to be more inclusive and allow anyone to connect to you, or more exclusive, and only allow true colleagues and friends.

2. Join at least six groups that are relevant to your profession, industry, and personal interests.

3. Create your own group. It is easy to start and manage LinkedIn groups, and this can get you a great deal of attention with a highly targeted audience.

4. Each group has its own discussion forum. Start answering other people's questions and post your own. This is a good way to get to know group members and you might even learn something in the process. If you pro-

vide relevant answers over time, you can be awarded with LinkedIn "expert" status.

5. Use the recommendation feature. Recommending others gains you exposure on their profile page. Likewise, you can ask others to recommend you. Do not neglect this because employers often review a potential candidate's profile and recommendations before making contact.

6. Update people on what you are working on. This only takes a few seconds and keeps you top of mind in your network.

7. Increase your visibility by making your profile public. This allows search engines to index your page.

8. Fill out your company profile and provide links to your blog and company Website.

9. Make use of your contacts. Find ways to keep in touch. Ask for referrals and do whatever else it takes to prevent these relationships from going stale.

Twitter – To Tweet or Not to Tweet

According to Mashable.com, the Social Media Guide (www.mashable. com), there are about 14 million Twitter users currently, and this number is growing about fifty percent per year. Twitter started more as a consumer medium but is now making major inroads to business marketing. A useful way to look at Twitter is to consider it a micro-blogging tool. Twitter posts (known as *tweets*) are limited to 140 characters of information, so you need to learn how to share information in very small bites, or use tweets to reference your blog or Website.

Just as with blogging and LinkedIn, there is little or no cost to use Twitter, other than the value of your time. However, you must make a time commitment, or Twitter will be a short-term experiment that will not benefit you. The basic idea is that you add followers to your own posts, and also follow others. You can make things happen very quickly, assuming you can acquire a large list of followers.

Here are some tips on how to get the most out of Twitter:

1. Have a unique brand. This is just as important on Twitter as in blogging. You have to stand out from the crowd.

2. Use it for quick marketing research. You can conduct an online poll and have the results in minutes, but you must keep it short.

3. Monitor your company name to learn what people are saying about you in real time. Do the same with your competitors. Many large companies such as Home Depot have one or more employees to monitor Twitter posts that reference their name.

4. Post only when you have something useful to say. Please resist the urge to post on inane subjects (e.g., what you had for breakfast), especially if you are using Twitter for business purposes.

5. You can create several tweets at once and pre-schedule them for specific times.

6. Never confuse tweeting with blogging. The 140-character tweet limit means that you should post only time-sensitive snippets and use your blog to develop topics in more detail.

7. If in doubt, do not tweet. Twitter is like email in that you can do a lot of damage if you hit the send button too quickly. People can search your tweets and everything you say can either add or subtract from your reputation. Just because Twitter is a fast and easy medium does not mean you should use it in a cavalier manner.

8. Be conversational. Twitter is a less formal medium, so do not be afraid to let your unique personality shine.

9. Publish your Twitter username on your blog, LinkedIn, and other social media accounts. Mine is @CRyanFusionMkt.

Success Tip: Get started in social media since it can have a large impact on your business.

Chapter 23

Launch Effective Email Campaigns

"In God we trust; all others we virus-scan."

–Unknown

Like many other business-to-business marketers, I have shifted a great deal of my promotional activities from traditional media to email over the past decade. B2B email has exploded, with total business email volume estimated at over 100 billion per day (according to McAfee). Unfortunately, spam makes up a large portion of that volume, with estimated spam rates ranging from a low of 79.5 percent as reported by MessageLabs Intelligence, to a high of 97 percent reported by Microsoft. Regardless of whether the number is 80 percent or 97 percent or somewhere in between, this is a huge problem for the B2B emailer.

Email has some great attributes that drive its growth. Outside of the cost of external list purchases and what you pay for a management tool, email is virtually free. You also get fantastic speed of execution—you can dream up a campaign in the morning and be receiving responses in the afternoon. And there is almost no medium that is more flexible. You can test offers, subject lines, body copy, and lists using small quantities, make the necessary changes based on test results, and launch the bulk of the campaign knowing you are putting your best foot forward.

The three most important keys to email success are first, to build a large and willing list of contacts who have opted in; second, to get your email delivered (avoiding the spam filters); and third, to give your prospects reasons to keep reading and responding to your messages. All of the following strategies relate to at least one of these three objectives.

Build a Strong Contact List

The ability to build a large and interested database of contacts is a skill that separates successful Fusion Marketers from the also-rans. A strong internal contact list will give you an extremely cost-effective way of generating leads and driving revenue. Email contact lists are an excellent way to keep in touch with prospects and nurture them until they are ready to engage in the sales process.

The secret to building your email database is to give your prospects free information that is valuable to them, without requesting anything in return other than a name and email address. Make sure that what you are giving away has a high perceived value, even if it costs you little or nothing to produce. A sales brochure does not have high perceived value, unlike a book or an informational paper on the best way to accomplish some particular business objective. Remember that you are investing in the future, not trying to sell the prospect on the first contact. You will get plenty of chances to sell later.

Permission in email can be either implicit or explicit. With implicit permission, you assume that anyone who has responded to one of your offers (e.g., attended an event or responded to a promotion) is okay with being on your email list. Explicit permission means that they have specifically agreed to receive email from you through an opt-in process. Also, make sure you clearly articulate your privacy policy. Let people know that you are not going to sell their email addresses to third parties, and they will be more likely to give you permission to send them email.

Whether you use the implicit or explicit strategy, make sure that you include a one-click "unsubscribe" link or button with every outgoing email. Do not try to be clever by making it difficult for the prospect to unsubscribe – this only breeds resentment. Resentful prospects not only don't buy things, they will identify you as a spam mailer to their email provider in order to stop your messages from getting through.

Ensure Email Delivery

You will become quite frustrated if a large percentage of your email ends up in your prospects' junk mail boxes. Spam filters are designed to capture true spam but they often block legitimate email as well. I have seen deliverability rates on individual emails range from forty percent up to ninety-eight percent. To prevent this from happening, make sure that your subject lines and body text do not mistakenly label your messages as spam. Avoid the type of language used by spammers, including words like *free, congratulations, winner, buy now, great offer, sweepstakes*, etc. You should also utilize one of the free spam checker products to validate the deliverability of your emails. One example is the Lyris ContentChecker service. You can find this tool and loads of other good resources at www.lyris.com.

Your choice of email format can also affect deliverability rates. HTML emails are far more attractive than plain text versions and work great as long as there are not issues that hamper readability. Design a couple of email templates that are proven to render correctly in different email clients and Web mail services, then use these formats repeatedly. However, keep in mind that many people view email messages on portable devices (PDAs) like iPhones and BlackBerrys, so make sure your formats render properly on these devices.

You may be tempted to mail to large quantities of people who have never opted-in to your contact list. This can get you blacklisted by the

ISPs and email providers, which means they will block any incoming email from your domain. Many of the compiled lists are *seeded* with email names designed to catch spammers. You will also be paying to reach non-existent prospects because delivery rates on these compiled lists are low, often with twenty to forty percent of the addresses invalid or expired.

Once you move from hundreds to thousands of contacts, it is a good idea to use email management software. This will help you with segmentation, templates, and deliverability. Three proven email management software tools are Silverpop Engage B2B (www.silverpop.com), Marketo (www.marketo.com), and Constant Contact (www.constantcontact.com). You should also review the automated email lead nurturing programs of SmartTracks (www.smarttracks.com) and Infusionsoft (www.infusionsoft.com).

Get Prospects to Open and Respond to Your Email

Remember that with email you are not competing just with your typical business enemies, but with *everyone* sending email to your prospects. Let us suppose you send an email to this humble author. On any given day, my business email volume runs between 125 and 175 messages. This is too many items crying out for my limited time and attention. How do I notice your message, let alone open and read it? Since you are a consumer as well as a marketer, consider what it takes to get *you* to notice one email over another in your cluttered email inbox.

Every person who receives your email will ask themselves two questions before they decide whether to open and read the message: Who sent me this, and what is it about? Here are some ways to get higher readership and response:

- Be forthright about your call to action. State what you want the email reader to do, and make sure your instructions are crystal clear. Remember that the burden of understandable communication is on you, not the recipient.

- Use a strong subject line. State a benefit. Arouse curiosity. Provoke. Hint at something great. Offer to solve a problem.

- Create a sense of urgency. Email has a short shelf life, sort of like the billboard you drive past on the highway. You read it and make a quick decision: should I move on to the next email, or consider this offer? Once you move on, there is little chance you will come back and respond.

- Pace yourself and don't ask for a major commitment too early in the relationship. For example, do not request a lot of data from the prospect if you only need their name and email address to start the communication process. Every bit of extra information you ask for will increase your abandonment rate.

- Many of your email recipients will have their preview panes enabled, so make sure the most enticing part of your copy shows up early.

- Instead of requiring the reader to click through to a separate form, include the response mechanism right in the email. If possible, pre-enter the person's name and email address. This one-click response capability will produce a higher response rate.

- Some B2B marketers claim that they get more response by sending their emails on Sundays, but I have found the best day to be Tuesday, followed by Wednesday and Thursday.

- Avoid using formatting like all capital letters, excessive exclamation points, or other symbols that make your email look like spam.

Success Tip: Build a large permission-based contact list to generate leads and customers at low cost.

Chapter 24

Generate Leads and Sales with Direct Mail

*"Marketing is what a company is in business to do.
Marketing is a company's ultimate objective."*

— Al Ries and Laura Ries

Direct mail may not be the medium of choice for today's B2B marketer, and in many cases, online and social media, particularly email, have proven more cost-effective. However, direct mail is still a significant part of the marketing mix for many companies, and other suppliers of direct marketing services say they use non-catalog direct mail, and nearly half (forty-six percent) say it is their primary channel for promotions. Therefore, direct mail does have an important role, either as a stand-alone marketing tool or as part of an integrated campaign. In fact, there are some distinct advantages direct mail has over other promotional media:

- It is highly targetable.

- It is less competitive.

- It may be the only way to reach certain people.

- It can be cost-effective.

- It is multi-dimensional.

- It is not email.

Direct mail does have its disadvantages. It is costly to reach each prospect, when compared to the cost of email and social media, especially since postal rates have increased so much over the past decade. Campaigns take much longer to execute than online campaigns and you may have to wait quite a while for response rate feedback. And many prospects have quit reading their promotional direct mail. Of course, it is also true that many have stopped reading promotional emails.

If you decide to incorporate direct mail as part of your promotional mix, pay special attention to acquiring mailing lists. Depending on the product and offer, up to fifty percent of a direct marketing campaign's effectiveness can be tied directly to the choice of target prospects. This is why, in the direct marketing industry, there is a saying, "The three most important factors in a direct marketing campaign are the list, the list, and the list." Not only do I agree, I would go so far as to say you can accomplish more by sending a mediocre direct mail package to a good list than you can by mailing the most clever and expensive package to a poor mailing list.

While many people know how to define their best prospects, they may not understand how to properly evaluate lists. Following are eight characteristics you should look for in a mailing list:

1. The list should contain individuals who match the profile of your existing customers.

2. The contacts should be available in sufficient quantities for you to accomplish your marketing objectives.

3. It should contain *fresh* names (those who have purchased or responded in the past six months).

4. The list should be clean and well-maintained and have only a small percentage of undeliverable addresses, guaranteed by the list owner.

5. It should allow for segmentation through selection options. Segmentation is a key skill of Fusion Marketing.

6. The list should be available for testing in small quantities. Most list owners require a minimum rental of 5,000 names, which is a good testing quantity.

7. The list has been used successfully for similar offers.

8. The rental price should be reasonable. Although novice marketers pay a great deal of attention to price, it is probably the least important factor. Differences in the response rates of direct mail lists are so great (particularly in business-to-business marketing) that a cost differential of ten, twenty, or even thirty dollars per thousand names is not likely to make or break a program.

Frankly, when it comes to mailing lists, there is a lot of junk on the market, so make sure you check references and have a guarantee of quality and deliverability. Your house list will generally be the cleanest and most responsive list, followed in order by competitors' lists, response lists, subscriber lists and finally, compiled lists. If the list has many names on it, try to arrange to first test small quantities in case the list is of poor quality.

Direct Mail Offers and Formats

Before you start on the creative portion of your direct mail campaign, make sure you have a good handle on your overall strategy and objectives. Tactics will be different depending on whether you are creating awareness, generating new leads, selling a product directly, or cross-selling existing customers. In many cases, it is okay to break even, or even lose money on a mailing, because new customers may have a lifetime value that makes it more important to gain the customer than to make a profit.

Next to the mailing list, the most important factor in direct mail success is the offer. Read the chapter on offers for some good ideas. The sole purpose of the offer is to motivate your prospect to take action. Good offers are compelling, timely, relevant to the audience, and easy to understand. They must also be simple for the prospect to take action on, since people will not go through a lot of trouble even if they are interested. Most often, you are better off presenting the prospect one offer at a time instead of multiple offers. Offers can be tested by dividing the mailing list and sending half the prospects offer "A" and the other half offer "B." This is known as *split testing*.

Once you select your target audience and have your objectives and offer specified, it is time to select a direct mail package format. *Format* refers to the structure of a direct mail package, including the letter and other components contained inside the envelope (printed or otherwise), as well as the outer envelope. Format also refers to the way the components are put together, including issues such as how and where specific components are personalized.

You should make the decision on which format to use based on numerous tangible and intangible factors, the most important of which is the audience. Who are the recipients of your mailing and to what do they respond? Another factor is the length of the message. What are you planning to say and how much room will you need to say it? Are you using the mailing to preserve an existing image or to promote a new one?

The actual physical size of the mailing is also important since certain formats lend themselves to large volumes and others to small volumes. Although direct mail experts may argue that no two packages are alike, there are formats used so often that they become almost standard. One of the most commonly used package formats consists of an outer en-velope, response form, business reply envelope (BRE), and a brochure or flyer. The outer envelope is always a key component of the package. While the envelope alone will not cause anyone to take action on your offer, unless your prospect opens the envelope, you have a zero percent chance of making a sale. Thus, the envelope has one primary purpose: to prompt your prospect to open it and read what's inside.

The closer the package looks to personal correspondence, the higher the response it will generate. This is true for both closed-face and window packages. Studies show that the average person takes only four to seven seconds to decide whether to open an envelope or toss it away. You have very little time to entice the reader inside the package, so try these techniques to get your packages opened and read:

- Consider a window envelope since they have higher open rates than non-window envelopes. Likewise, large envelopes have higher open rates.

- Use commemorative stamps or multiple postage stamps.

- Don't be too predictable. If you always send your mail in white number ten envelopes, switch to a different size or color, or try a self-mailer.

- Use a curiosity provoker, such as a quiz that starts on the envelope and carries through to the internal pack-age copy.

- Place copy and graphics on the back as well as the front of the envelope.

- Write a strong benefit statement on the envelope.

- Offer a glimpse of your key visual or product through a window in the envelope. (Curiosity is a strong motivator).

Sales letters are the most important components in direct mail packages, because this is where you either convince the prospect to respond or lose her. Try these tips for a more effective direct mail letter:

- Use a "P.S." Studies show that the postscript is often read before the body copy of the letter. Keep the P.S. to twenty-five words or less.

- Have a credible individual (with legible handwriting) sign the letter. After reading the salutation, readers usually look to see who signed the letter.

- A two-color letterhead out pulls one-color.

- Illustrations or photos on letters can increase response.

- Use, but don't overdo: underlining, bold type, and handwriting in the margins.

- Use subheads to break up long text.

Each prospect has a preferred method of responding to a direct mail offer. While many prefer the convenience of a toll-free 800 number, many others prefer to respond via a Web form or postal mail. For mail responders, you need to provide a reply device of some type. A Business Reply Card (BRC) or Business Reply Envelope (BRE) is your best bet. You use a BRC to collect exactly the same information that you request on a Web response form.

Reply devices are not limited to simple response cards and envelopes. Coupons, surveys, mock invoices, certificates, sweepstakes entry forms, and a hundred other formats have been successfully used. Each of these formats can be personalized with all or part of the information contained in the prospect's database record. If possible, have the prospect's name and address filled in, since this will usually boost response.

You can also repeat the offer on the reply form or use it to re-state the major benefit. If the form is large enough, include a tear-off stub which repeats the offer and/or serves as the customer's receipt. A large reply form can show an illustration or photo of the product. Above all, make sure your ordering instructions are crystal clear. And please leave plenty of room for the customer to fill in his name, address, and credit card information.

You have several other options for direct mail package formats. Self-mailers are inexpensive and can be very effective for certain types of offers. The term *self-mailer* is used because this format needs no outer envelope to carry its message. Usually, the self-mailer also contains its own response vehicle, in the form of an attached or bound-in BRC.

In a six-panel brochure, one panel can serve as the headline or billboard which states the major benefit; three more panels can be devoted to supporting copy and a call to action; and one panel can be used for the respondent to fill in return address information. The final panel is used for the mailer's business reply permit information.

Postcards are proven B2B mailing formats that are even less expensive than self-mailers. They are particularly effective for promoting registrations at sales seminars, for generating leads, and for other applications where the message is concise. Single postcards are great when you have a simple offer and want to capture all your lead information via phone or a Web form. Double-postcards use two panels for headlines and supporting copy, one panel for the responder to fill in contact information, and the final panel for the mailer's business reply permit information.

Packages with a unique format serve a purpose when you are communicating to a very important or highly targeted audience. Examples of specialty formats include die-cut brochures, pop-up devices, boxes, DVDs, advertising specialties (such as pens, calendars, etc.), and telegrams. Many specialty formats are also known as *dimensional* mailers because they have greater depth and substance than traditional mailing packages.

More Strategies for Direct Mail Success

Here are eight additional ways to ensure fantastic results with your direct mail programs:

1. Practice repetition. Campaigns that include multiple mailings usually work better than single mailing programs.

2. Fish when the fish are biting. January, February, and October tend to produce the best direct mail response rates. The worst months to mail are May, June, and July (probably due to vacation schedules).

3. Always test your campaign on smaller quantities before attacking the entire prospect universe.

4. Make sure you thoroughly understand the characteristics of your target audience and what motivates them to take action.

5. Never undertake a direct mail program without specific and measurable objectives.

6. Spend a lot of time developing a unique and compelling offer. The only thing more important than the offer is your choice of mailing lists.

7. Make sure your direct mail reinforces the rest of your marketing activities.

8. Work with direct mail experts. Most general ad agen-

cies know little about direct mail, and much of what they think they know is wrong or out of date.

Speaking of experts, there are some great resources available to help you manage the entire direct mail process. One that I mentioned earlier is called SmartTracks (smarttracks.com)— an automated system that can handle everything from prospect identification to mailing format, creative, and tracking response rates.

Success *Tip:* Direct mail can be an important part of an integrated marketing strategy.

Chapter 25

Optimize Marketing Events

"Much like any other advertising medium, a trade show lets people know who you are and what you do."

–Dick Wheeler

Trade shows and industry conferences are not always the most effective ways to get your message across or to generate leads. Attendance is down at most B2B shows and there are more efficient ways to reach your prospects at lower cost. Yet, for many organizations, trade shows are considered an essential part of the marketing mix. If your industry has a well-developed network, people could view your company's absence at the big annual conference as a sign that you are in trouble. In such an industry, even if you feel the event is not the best use of your company's marketing dollars, you are forced to go back year after year.

Here are eight reasons to consider adding trade shows to your marketing arsenal:

1. Companies usually send their decision-makers to trade shows, particularly in tough economic times. As long as you choose the right places to exhibit, the leads you generate should be of decent quality.

2. If you conduct most of your business by telephone or email, or have a widely dispersed customer base, trade shows may be the only opportunity you have to meet and greet your customers and prospects.

3. If your competition exhibits at a particular trade show, you may wish to do so as a defensive measure. You don't want your customers and prospects exposed to the competition's products without also having the benefit of your presence.

4. Trade shows are excellent forums to present new product ideas, and provide you the opportunity to field-test products and services before committing large sums to marketing and sales programs.

5. Trade shows are great opportunities to make important contacts with industry colleagues, suppliers, partners, and association leaders.

6. Industry press, financial press, and analysts routinely attend large conferences and trade shows. These events can be your best opportunity to catch so many analysts, editors, and reporters at one time in one place.

7. Your competitors probably use trade shows to introduce new products and services. For this reason, such events provide an outstanding opportunity to conduct competitive marketing research. You can learn a lot just by walking around and asking questions.

8. Although it is usually not a primary purpose of trade shows, you can sometimes conduct new business at these events. In high-ticket industries, it is not unusual

for one deal made at a trade show to more than pay
the entire cost of exhibiting.

While fewer in number than past years, trade show attendees are better educated, come from higher levels in their organizations, and are
much more serious about the business purpose of the event than in
the past. In short, there are fewer tire-kickers and more buyers. These
changes are definitely good news for the exhibitor, but you must respond to them by changing your perceptions and methods. Treat each
person who visits your booth with greater respect, reflecting his or her
increased value, and be willing to spend the extra time and energy required to convince a more skeptical and serious prospect.

Setting Trade Show Objectives

Many organizations have poor experiences with trade shows because
they lack a professional approach to preparing for the events. It is the
planning you do before the show that determines your success. As a
results-driven marketer, you will want to start by establishing specific
objectives for each trade show. And by setting objectives, I don't mean
"getting a bunch of leads" or "meeting new prospects." Rather, you
should be very specific in each of the following areas that apply to your
situation:

- Dollar volume of sales. As I noted above, even shows
  focused on generating leads can sometimes produce
  significant sales revenue. If this is your intention, by all
  means quantify the amount of sales that you intend to
  achieve.

- Generating a specific number of leads. Goals should be
  set for the total number of leads, and should also be bro-

ken down to account for lead quality. For instance, it is easy to come up with a gimmick that will get a large number of people to let you scan their badges or drop their business cards into your *fishbowl*. However, the majority of these so-called leads will not even be suspects so you need a way to quickly separate the wheat from the chaff.

- The average dollar cost for each qualified lead. To compute this figure, total all costs associated with the show and divide by the number of leads you intend to generate.

- Meetings with qualified prospects. Because you are likely to have one or more of your senior managers in attendance, trade shows offer a good opportunity to conduct working meetings (perhaps meetings where sales are closed) with local prospects or those who have also traveled to the event.

- Meetings with selected media and analysts. Press and analyst meetings are an extremely valuable use of a marketing manager's time. These should be scheduled weeks before the event. Although it is sometimes possible to arrange these meetings at the show itself, editors are so busy it is more fruitful to pre-plan. Remember that editors and reporters have one thing in common with you: they eat. Take advantage of this fact by inviting editors and analysts for breakfast, lunch, or a cup of coffee.

- Getting on the podium. Work hard to get a speaking slot for yourself or one of your executives. This will give you a great deal of credibility and drive additional traffic to your booth.

Once you have set objectives for the trade show in these six areas, make sure each person who attends from your company is well aware of his or her specific role in making the goals a reality.

How to Generate High Quality Trade Show Leads

So you've made the decision to bite the bullet and spend anywhere from a few thousand to tens of thousands of dollars to exhibit at a particular show. You will want to make sure you have done everything possible to generate a large number of high quality leads. As stated earlier, lead quantity and lead quality are often two very different things. Consider this point carefully, because the type of program you develop to attract large numbers of people to your booth will be very different from that required to attract quality prospects.

If you are going for the *quality* model, you might want to forget the giveaways, games, or contests that are designed solely to attract the greatest number of people to your booth, regardless of their need for, or interest in, your product and company. What you often get with a quantity-based approach are large numbers of people looking to fill their bags with the largest amount of goodies possible before the exhibit hall closes.

Attracting large numbers of people to your booth is not wrong but most often, it is more important to get the right people to your booth. One technique that helps accomplish this purpose is the pre-show email or direct mail. Contact the organization sponsoring the show and ask them to send you a list of registrants. Timing is very important. The trick is to make the request in plenty of time to get a promotion out before the show, yet not so early that you miss a large number of late registrants.

While there are many choices as to what you can send, I suggest you make it a coupon or gift certificate that is redeemable only at your booth. The certificate should be for something of reasonable value. If you've selected your audience carefully, you will find it more effective to spend the same amount of money providing decent gifts to smaller numbers of qualified prospects, instead of cheap trinkets for large numbers of unqualified people (again, the quality vs. quantity approach).

You can also call to invite important prospects to visit your booth when one or more of your senior managers will be there. Your call could go something like: "Mr. Smith, our company president would like to meet you at the show and buy you a cup of coffee. He is very interested in hearing your opinions on our new product line." This type of call can be flattering to the prospect and is a very effective way to increase sales.

There are two keys to making a giveaway program work. First, the gift item should have some connection with your product or service. The second key is to require something more than the individual's presence in return for the gift. For instance, you can require the prospect to fill out a short questionnaire at your booth, which asks about his use of, and interest in, the type of products or services you offer. The amount of information you can collect will be directly proportional to the value of the gift you are offering.

If this is starting to sound like a blatant attempt to purchase information about your prospects, you are right on target. The primary purpose of exhibiting at a trade show is to gather information on your qualified prospects, not to feed them information about you. While this goes against the natural instincts of many salespeople, it is true.

Do not make the mistake of giving the trade show leads to sales reps until you have captured them electronically. Otherwise, you may never see them again. They will be swallowed up in the sales reps' own prospect files, lost to the marketing department forever. Be aggressive about your follow-up after the show. Prospects have a short memory when it comes to the booths they visited.

How to Use Web Seminars to Generate Business

Web seminars (or Webcasts if you prefer) are a great way to generate leads and customers. They are also a great way to increase awareness, move prospects to the next stage of the selling cycle, and build the database. They have a relatively low cost per prospect and give you a wide geographic reach from the comfort of your Web browser and telephone. I have been using these types of events for over ten years and as a result, I have generated tens of thousands of leads and millions of dollars of sales.

Web event marketing makes sense if:

- You have a dispersed audience

- You lack critical mass in local markets

- Your target audience is technology savvy

- Your product is priced in the mid- to upper-range

- You want to create a series of events

- Executives are your primary audience or are crucial to the purchase decision

- You have access to a good prospect list

- You have a compelling reason for people to attend

- You have a way to sustain the relationship after the event

Web events may not be right for you if you sell a low-cost or commodity product that you cannot differentiate from your competition, or if you have a very small budget.

People attend Web events for a variety of reasons. Some want to gain competitive intelligence and others just want general information about your product category. You will have to pay for the latter group even though they are not truly prospects. However, others will attend to get information about your product or service or to confirm a decision to either purchase from you or a competitor. To reach your goals with these people you will need to present content that is relevant, timely, and unique. The topic is even more important than your choice of speakers, and if you are offering material your prospects can't get elsewhere, so much the better. When you write the invitation, visualize your prospect sitting at her desk and deciding: *Is what I am going to learn in this event worth the investment of a half-hour or an hour of my valuable time?*

Just as with other types of marketing programs, you will receive a full spectrum of inquiries from Web events. While results vary depending on company and offer, here is a distribution of lead quality from fifteen Web seminars I held recently.

A Leads = 154 = 8% of total
B Leads = 231 = 12% of total
C/D Leads = 652 = 34% of total
Dead or Unknown = 883 = 46% of total

The fifteen events cost approximately $22,500, a relatively low cost because the company had a large house list that generated most of the registrants. We generated the 385 high-quality A and B leads at a cost of only $58 each, a tiny fraction of the average sales price of $15,000. The 652 C/D leads will be nurtured over time and can be expected to produce an additional 150-plus A and B leads. Most important, we paid for the entire campaign with the first two sales, so it was highly profitable. This campaign was a perfect example of how to use Fusion Marketing principles at every step in the process.

Here are some valuable pointers for conducting successful Web events:

1. To attract a crowd, you must have a compelling topic and a qualified speaker.

2. Make sure you send a confirmation email immediately upon registration.

3. Follow up via email and phone one or two days before the live event.

4. Make the event as interactive as possible. Allow questions at the end.

5. Have a few pre-written questions to get the Q&A session off to a good start.

6. If you only have a few people on the line, do not let the other attendees know this. Make them feel that they are part of a large group learning about a hot topic.

7. Contact attendees within forty-eight hours of the end of event. Have a real offer, instead of just asking: *How did you like the event and what can we do for you?*

8. Call and email the *no-shows*. Send them a link to the presentation. You can often get as many good leads from the no-shows as you do the attendee pool.

9. Be willing to make mistakes. I have made many over the years. You will get better at conducting successful events over time.

10. Never be afraid to copy a good idea.

Closely related to the Web seminar is the telephone seminar. Here you give the presentation to the prospects without the benefit of the computer presentation and/or demonstration. Telephone seminars are easier to manage than Web events but it is harder to hold the attention of prospects without visual support.

A new type of marketing event that you should consider is the virtual conference or trade show, which is a hybrid between a live event and Web seminar. These events can include all or some of the following: online presentations, auditorium, exhibit hall, chat room, video greetings from exhibitors, private messages, document library, and giveaways – many of the same features you find at live conferences. For example, I just attended the *Leading Edge B2B Marketing Virtual Conference* with 4,500 other participants. You may not have the resources to produce such an event, but you can start by being an online exhibitor. A company called ON24 provides a platform for organizing and conducting virtual events.

Using Sales Seminars

I have had very good success with live sales seminars over the years but their effectiveness is waning, primarily because prospects can easily get the same type of information from Web-based seminars. If you think in-person events can work for your business, it is certainly worth testing.

Seminars fall into two general categories: those that support the sale of goods and services and those that run as a separate profit center. For our purposes, we will focus on the former type of event. Here are some reasons you might want to make seminars an integral part of your marketing program:

- Seminars put you directly in front of your prospects, which may be the only time you are getting a chance to see them face-to-face.

- Seminar attendees tend to be well qualified. Very few people will sit through a two-to-four-hour presentation unless they are interested in the subject matter.

- For complex products, or for those with long sales cycles, seminars can move attendees up the selling continuum. Suspects become prospects, prospects become hot prospects, and hot prospects become buyers. Sales can be closed in a much shorter time by adding seminars to the marketing mix.

- Professionally conducted seminars increase your organization's credibility in the marketplace. But you must be careful, because mediocre seminars will have a negative effect on your credibility.

- Seminars give you an excellent opportunity to conduct primary marketing research since they provide a captive audience of qualified prospects.

- Seminars can change the dynamics of the seller/buyer relationship. If you have provided prospects with valuable information, hosted them in comfort for several hours, and made the experience a pleasant one, a certain bond is forged that transcends typical buyer/seller relationships, and this can work to your advantage.

While this list of benefits sounds tempting, conducting seminars also poses several possible problems. First, seminar programs can be expensive. While there are low-cost ways of marketing and conducting seminars, these programs can be expensive compared to other marketing methods. The cost is not only financial, since creating and implementing seminars takes valuable staff time.

Tips on Conducting a Winning Seminar

To help make your seminar program a success, make sure your program is informational, not sales-oriented. You will earn more brownie points (and sales) from your audience if you approach the seminar as a chance to share expertise and help your attendees. There are exceptions to this rule, such as when your products are unique and interesting enough to serve as the basis for the presentation. And it goes without saying that in a free seminar, a small amount of self-promotion is tolerated. But outside these constraints, don't insult your audience by turning your seminar into a sales pitch.

The program should be interesting and informative. Whatever you can do to add entertainment value will be appreciated by the audience, particularly if the program content is dry or highly technical. A little tasteful humor never hurts.

Consider asking one of your best customers to appear on the program and explain how your product or service has been helpful. As the saying goes, "It ain't bragging if someone else says it about you." But make sure you have a good idea of what the customer will say. You don't want any surprises here, such as the customer mentioning that he also likes your competitor's product.

If you can, use audio/visuals to highlight the important points. Most people don't want to sit through a half-day or full-day lecture. PowerPoint has become a standard, and video can be a major plus.

Most importantly, do not forget to rehearse. If you have more than one person on the program, ask all speakers to rehearse individually. However, don't settle for only individual rehearsals. Always have at least one full run-through several days before the seminar to see how well the total program works. Sometimes you will find that one of your speakers is totally unprepared, or has a very different idea of how to present the material.

Two schools of thought exist about whether to charge people to attend sales seminars. The first says that because you are providing valuable information, you should be compensated for the value of that information. Another argument is that charging an admission fee also discourages the unqualified freeloaders who show up at seminars just to get a free meal and competitors who show up to make contact with your prospects and customers.

There are three good reasons *not* to charge a fee. First, most people will not sit through an hours-long program just to get a free meal. They will have at least moderate interest in the subject matter. This doesn't mean that everyone will buy what you are selling now, but many will turn out to be viable future prospects. As for competitors, simply do not allow them to attend. It is your party and you can invite or un-invite anyone you want.

Reason two for not charging is that many qualified prospects who would otherwise attend, will not do so if they are charged a fee. This is particularly true if your audience consists of low- to mid-level personnel. Although they are often decision influencers and recommenders, they must get approval from their superiors to attend a fee-based seminar.

Reason three is that most people attend sales seminars because they believe they will learn something of value to help them in their personal or professional lives. If the seminar is free, they expect a certain amount of sales information about the sponsoring company and its products or services which they would not tolerate if they were forced to pay a fee.

Given the arguments on both sides, your decision should be one of economics. If the potential exists for generating significant revenue in your primary business from the prospects who attend, then you should consider a free seminar. However, if you can't pay for the seminar program from product and service sales, you should charge a fee, or find other ways to promote your organization.

Success Tip: Consider adding Web, telephone, live and virtual seminars to your marketing mix.

Chapter 26

Increase Awareness with Public Relations

"Some are born great, some achieve greatness, and some hire public relations officers."

– Daniel J. Boorstin

If you are on the lead generation side of the marketing department, you have probably wondered, "Just what are those PR people doing and how are they helping us?" They seem to spend their time writing press releases and talking to analysts, but they don't really appear to accomplish anything! If you are wondering this, the CFO probably has the same questions. In my experience, only a small minority of organizations have a good handle on just what they are getting in return for their PR expenditures.

Instead of viewing PR as a separate and distinct part of the marketing operation, begin to consider it as a critical component of the end-to-end process. The PR team has a lot to add and they can accelerate your results if you get everyone thinking about the benefits of integrated marketing. To start creating synergy, look for ways to bring PR into the integrated marketing mix and drop any barriers that exist between the

PR and marketing teams. Also look for ways to leverage the content that the PR folks create in your marketing programs.

Press releases are the backbone of public relations because they are highly informational and tell an ongoing story of the organization's progress (or lack thereof). Think of your press releases as pieces of a larger puzzle, each one of which provides part of the overall perspective. For this reason, you should keep your press releases brief and to the point. They work best, and are published more often, when they are factual instead of sales-oriented, and concise instead of wordy. Make sure to optimize your releases for search engines by including keyword rich copy and links back to your Website.

Remember that press releases are also referred to as *news releases* for a reason – they are supposed to be about news. Here are some legitimate topics for press releases:

- Launch of a new product or upgrade to a new version.

- Compelling story about a customer buying or using your products or services.

- Good results achieved by a customer or partner.

- Winning a product or company award.

- Major promotions or personnel additions, particularly at the executive level.

- Strategic partnership deals.

- Community service projects supported by the company.

- Whatever else you think of that is newsworthy.

How PR Can Make a Big Difference

Elsewhere in this book, I have talked about the concept of both push marketing and pull marketing. Push marketing occurs when you reach out to prospects, regardless of their current interest in your product or service, and attempt to convince them to engage in the sales process with you. By contrast, pull marketing occurs when you make it easy for those who already know they have a need for what you offer. In the first instance, your job is to find the prospect and in the second, your job is to make it easy for the prospect to find you. To put it another way, push marketers use a hammer and pull marketers use a magnet.

Public relations can help with both push and pull programs. While PR is usually better at creating awareness than in generating leads directly, you will often get actionable leads from a clever and well-executed PR campaign. For many companies, the barrier is not in selling enough prospects they have engaged with, but rather in finding enough prospects to engage. When the prospect is interested, either because he or she remembers you from the press release, article, news story or analyst's report, you are more likely to gain consideration than if you are unknown to the prospect. That is the essence of the PR strategy—creating awareness, spreading the message, and preparing the groundwork for future sales.

Consider expanding your target audience with your PR strategy and messaging. In addition to the usual targets of press and analysts, make sure you also include:

1. Employees – Although they are often overlooked, employees should never be taken for granted. They can do more to help you, or hurt you, than any other group. Companies with excellent PR programs find it easier to attract the most qualified new employees. Your employees are also excellent barometers of the credibility of your message.

2. Customers – They are always an important segment of your public. Their opinion of your products and services is paramount because their willingness to spend money is what allows you to exist. However, you must remember that the message you send to your customers must be accurate. You cannot fool customers, because they start with a base of knowledge about your company.

3. Prospects – Public relations can be a powerful weapon in the effort to turn prospects into customers. You can divide prospects into subgroups by industry, size, type of products purchased, and other criteria.

4. Stockholders – Whether you are a public or private company, investors have a large stake in the success of your organization. You cannot assume their continued allegiance, however. Witness the financial losses and plunging stock prices faced by organizations that receive unfavorable publicity.

5. Industry Leaders – Every industry has a small number of individuals who have the capacity to influence large numbers of others. I call these people *opinion leaders* because the opinions they express today often become standard industry dogma tomorrow. Industry leader segments include association leaders, authors, public speakers, editors, known innovators, and heads of large companies. Building relationships with the right industry leaders can do more for you and your organization than mailing tons of press releases.

6. Community and Government – Most organizations depend on the loyalty and support of people in the local

community. It is a good idea to have community leaders and the local, state, and federal governments on your side.

Send your press releases, articles, relevant blog postings, and other announcements to these groups to keep them in the loop with what you are doing.

Measuring the Value of Your PR Efforts

Most companies have no idea what impact PR has on their lead and sales results. With the many analytics tools available, there is no longer an excuse for a lack of measurement. Here are some of the items you will want to capture.

1. Growth in awareness.

2. Stickiness of the message.

3. Competitive placement.

4. Website hits. Strong outreach programs will cause a measurable boost in hits to your Website. I have seen PR campaigns cause a spike of 100 percent or more in Web traffic over a period of days.

5. Leads. While you will get many hits on your Website where the source is tough to measure, make sure that your CRM system or marketing automation system contains a separate lead source for PR activities that are measurable. For example, if you run an article under one of your executive's bylines, include a simple but identifiable URL at the end of the article, perhaps offering a white paper or other free information. This URL should direct the prospect to a landing page that

will capture the PR-driven lead source, as well as information about the prospect.

The first three items are soft measures, which show how you are remembered and/or perceived by the target audience, while the last two are behavioral metrics, showing what prospects actually did as a result of exposure to the program. One of the easiest and fastest ways to capture PR-related data is through online survey tools such as SurveyMonkey. If you have (or can rent) email addresses for the target audience, it is possible to create a survey, launch the survey, and measure the results, in just a few days. Once you have the initial survey complete and tabulated, you can use the results as a benchmark to measure progress or (hopefully not) lack of progress.

Behavioral metrics are easier to measure because you can use common business tools to monitor these metrics. You can use your CRM system to capture leads and you can measure Website traffic with several tools, including Google Analytics, WebCEO, and VisiStat.

Outside-the-Box PR Strategies

Make it personal – There are two important ways to make your PR personal. First, by the tone of your communications focusing on the human side of your target audience. Communicate in the spirit of a person talking to another person, not as a company talking to nameless and faceless prospects. The second part of being personal is to base your PR on a key executive who has special and acknowledged expertise in your chosen market.

Make it fun – People like to do business with people they like. One of the best examples of a fun personality combined with great business acumen is Herbert D. Kelleher, founder of Southwest Airlines. When asked what made Southwest Airlines unique, Mr. Kelleher answered, "What's special about Southwest Airlines? Our people...anybody can buy the tangibles, but nobody can replicate the intangibles very easily. And I'm talking about the joie de vivre—the spirit of our people." Although Mr. Kelleher has retired from the airline, you can tell that his spirit carries on when you take a flight on Southwest.

Make it unique – Make sure your PR strategy is in complete alignment with your differentiation and unique selling proposition. People notice uniqueness far more easily than me-too-ism. Uniqueness also sells, and it often sells at a premium price.

Make it sticky – Stickiness refers to messages that are memorable. There are two ways to aid stickiness: first with a unique and powerful message, and second with a good message repeated over and over again.

Persist – Many companies practice just enough PR to say they have done it, but a paucity of PR will have little or no impact. A press release every six months is not going to cut it. Send news out on a regular basis or the (old) news section of your Website will make you look stale.

Use social networking – There are many social media tools available to help you move the needle of public perception, and gain far more awareness among your target audience. For example, a blog is a great way for reporters, editors, and analysts to find you and get the word out about your company and products.

Search term alignment – Coordinate your search engine optimization (SEO) and pay per click strategies with your public relations messages. Include key search terms in the text of every press release.

Get published – There is something about the written word that adds to an individual's credibility and reputation. The greatest credibility builder is to publish a book. All you need to get started is special knowledge in your field of expertise and a unique way of presenting your information. If you do not have the time and material for a book, at least publish articles.

Self-promote – Get your name out there with public speaking, presentations, podcasts, articles, blogs, LinkedIn, etc. If it helps the company, create your own brand and establish thought leadership.

> **Success Tip:** Aggressive public relations can have an enormous impact on awareness and lead generation.

Chapter 27

Build a Powerful Marketing Database

*"Your own customer list is the best in the world—but
only if it bulges with information about each customer."*
— Guerrilla Marketing's Golden Rule # 5

atabase marketing combines technology (your database) with
traditional direct marketing techniques. Most organizations have
several databases (e.g., customers, vendors, purchase transactions).
However, marketing databases are designed for specific purposes and
have the following criteria:

- The database allows for easy entry of names and addresses of customers and/or prospects (hopefully at
  the point of sale or inquiry). This is the simplest of criteria and it is the reason many contact management
  systems refer to themselves as databases.

- All known relevant information about customers and
  prospects, including demographics, response history,
  purchasing history, and contact history is contained in
  the database. When you have a means for collecting
  and storing such information, you are building a *knowl-*

edge base. The larger this reservoir of knowledge, the greater the potential for your marketing programs.

- The information contained in the database can be used to construct a profile of customers and prospects. Such a profile minimizes marketing efforts aimed at unqualified prospects, and forms the basis of defining potential new audience segments.

- The database can be segmented for target marketing purposes. Without the ability to select subsets of the database, you will be severely handicapped.

- The database provides full access to customer and prospect data at every level at which the data is used (marketing, sales, customer service, finance).

- The database consolidates redundant data and automatically flags duplicate entries.

- The database is scalable. This means that it should accommodate growth in the amount of data and number of users, with no changes in basic technology or procedures.

- The database facilitates communications between your organization and your prospects and customers. These communications can then be used to gather more relevant information, in a continual cycle of renewal.

Ten Profitable Ways to Use a Database Marketing System

Database marketing can increase your marketing effectiveness in the following areas:

1. Target Marketing – Information contained in the database can be used to include those prospects and customers most likely to purchase a particular product, and exclude those unlikely to purchase.

2. Test Marketing – By strictly defining and controlling those who are exposed to a promotional message in small quantities (at low cost), you can make inferences about the effect of that message on larger audiences.

3. Marketing Research – Provided you enter an adequate quality and quantity of information into your database, you can use it to learn a great deal about the characteristics, needs, and interests of your marketplace.

4. Upgrading and Cross-Selling Customers – Once patterns of purchase behavior are discovered, customers can be upgraded to new products, and cross sold add-on products.

5. Deleting Unprofitable Customers – By maintaining full purchase history data on your customers, you can delete those who prove consistently unprofitable. Likewise, you can identify and delete unresponsive prospect segments. Sometimes it is wise to delete an entire audience segment, in order to concentrate limited resources where they will do the most good.

6. Keeping in Touch – A database allows you to maintain

contact with your customers and prospects, even when you do not have the time to stay in touch personally.

7.   Personalizing Communications – Variable information contained in the database allows you to talk to your customers based on their past purchasing behavior.

8.   Building Relationships – Entering a prospect/customer into the database brings him into your circle of marketing influence. You can use the database to create, build, and maintain ongoing two-way communications with prospects and customers.

9.   Improving Your Image – In addition to prospects and customers, you can use your database to maintain contact with other groups important to your success, including press, analysts, industry leaders, trade and professional association leaders, suppliers, and employees.

10. Generating Inexpensive Leads – At my last two high-technology companies, I was able to build one database from 15,000 names to over 80,000, and the other from 4,000 to over 60,000 contacts. Both of these remarket databases became valuable resources to the companies, and were a great source of additional low-cost leads and sales.

Type of Information to Capture in the Database

No matter how well designed the technology, every B2B database is only as good as the data it contains. You want the system to capture as much of the data as possible through prospect or customer interaction. Here are some of the general data categories:

Transaction data – This is the easiest data to obtain, since you are already collecting it in some form. Transaction data refers to what the customer purchased, and includes the timing of the purchase, the payment method used, and how he or she contacted you (e.g., email, phone, walk-in, or interactive).

Response data – As the name implies, you capture response data every time a customer or prospect makes contact with your company for any reason. This response could result in a sale, or it could be an information request, complaint, account query, etc. It is important to track every inquiry to a promotion by lead source since this is useful intelligence that will help you sell.

Personal demographics – This type of data provides a picture of your customers and prospects outside of their experiences with you. Personal demographic characteristics include age, gender, residence, marital status, presence of children, income, and education. Demographic data can be overlaid onto existing data but it can be highly inaccurate if it is based on geographic location, rather than known specifics about an individual.

Business demographics – This data is similar to personal demographics but concerns the prospect at work and his or her business, including title, company name, size, industry type, location, company structure, finances, and management.

Psychographic data – Psychographic information can also be termed *lifestyle* or *preference* data. It refers to the customer's likes, dislikes, interests, and habits.

Industry specific data – This type of data comes from secondary re-

search sources, and includes general market statistics, compiled response data, and data extrapolated from government or industry databases or publications.

The Database Building Process

The following three graphics illustrate how the database building process works over time.

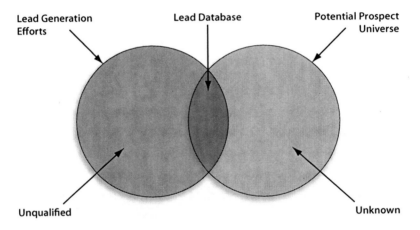

Database Building: Early Stages

In the early stages of database building, you know that a universe of
potential prospects exists, but you have had contact with very few of
them. Your database is small but you are determined to grow it into a
valuable marketing asset.

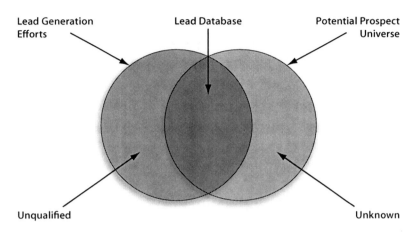

Database Building: Middle Stages

During the middle stages of the process, you continue reaching out to the prospect universe with various offers—some informational and some for lead generation. As more people respond, your database grows and you are able to generate leads from your internal prospect list as well as external lists. Your lead nurturing program is working well and your cost per inquiry has decreased substantially.

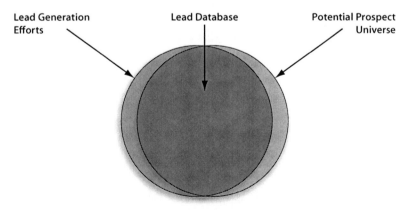

Database Building: Later Stages

Over the course of a few years, you have built an impressive database—perhaps the finest in your industry. You are required to do fewer lead generation campaigns to the prospect universe because you already have a majority of these contacts in your own house file. Your cost per lead is very low and the quality of leads is high because you have been practicing Fusion Marketing lead nurturing strategies. Your database is now an essential component of your unstoppable marketing and sales machine.

Strategies for Successful Database Marketing

As I have demonstrated, efficient database marketing can have many benefits to your organization. Follow these best practices to achieve the best possible results from your database marketing programs:

1. Take it seriously – You can build a powerful database-marketing file and use it to generate leads and revenue, but you need to establish objectives and diligently apply the strategies in this chapter.

2. Build your own list – There are many opportunities to buy so-called qualified lists. Most of the time, these people are not good prospects. They do not know you and have no desire to hear from you. They will often view your communications as spam or junk mail. It is better to build a database of those who have responded to you and are okay with being contacted.

3. Capture data automatically – Most successful B2B companies are using the Web to generate interest and capture lead information. Make sure you are able to import the data directly into your CRM or contact management system—not only the original inquiry, but also all subsequent inquiries.

4. Maintain all relevant data – Really think about the information you are going to keep on your prospects and customers. Make sure that you have a use for what you keep. Likewise, make sure you capture all necessary data from the beginning because it can be difficult to add it later. If you focus your marketing efforts on on-line media, the most important piece of data to capture is email addresses.

5. Make it easy for people to opt in and opt out – Of course you want to give prospects many opportunities to become part of your database. However, you should also make it very easy for them to opt out of future communications.

6. Append data – If your list is missing important information, you can often acquire it through appending services.

7. Keep your list clean – No one likes to get multiple emails, postal mailings, or phone solicitations. You should keep your own file clean of duplicates, but also practice merge/purge to eliminate duplicates on any rental lists you use. The greater the similarity between the rental lists and your house list, the higher the percentage of likely duplicates.

8. Maintain your remarket list in one data format – Try not to keep your data in separate files and if necessary, migrate and transform the data on multiple lists to a common format.

9. Give people reasons to stay with you – If you want to minimize opt-outs, make sure that all of your communications are not of the hard-sell variety. Mix in some non-

selling communications in the form of articles, industry updates, online events, and perhaps a newsletter.

Success Tip: Build a large database of prospects and use that database to make relevant offers that move these prospects further in the sales cycle.

Chapter 28

Drive Revenue with Effective Telephone Techniques

"Telephone: An invention of the devil which abrogates some of the advantages of making a disagreeable person keep his distance."

– Ambrose Bierce

The telephone's role in business-to-business marketing and sales has changed dramatically in the past few years. I believe that the telephone is declining as a significant direct sales and lead generation tool, but it still has a substantial role to play in lead qualification and nurturing. B2B marketers are using the telephone for these purposes:

1. Direct sale of products and services – Companies have used telemarketing to successfully sell products ranging from information costing a few dollars to financial investments and computer software costing over $100,000.

2. Upgrading current customers – Telemarketing is an ex-

cellent way to keep in touch with existing customers, cross-sell new products and services, and increase the average order size for products and services.

3. Generating leads – You can use telemarketing to contact raw leads on outside mailing lists and convert these suspects into bona fide prospects. You can then follow up these new prospects with other marketing methods such as email or personal selling. I do not usually recommend telemarketing for this purpose but some companies are doing it effectively.

4. Reactivating stagnant accounts – This is a great use of the telephone. Former customers, members, and donors are often neglected. This is unfortunate because they are an excellent source of revenue and it is usually easier and more cost-effective to revive an inactive account than to gain a new one.

5. Generating attendance at trade shows and seminars – Telemarketing is a good method of filling free and fee-based seminars and can help you sell exhibit space and registrations at trade shows and conferences. It is more effective if the phone call is following up an email or direct mail solicitation.

6. Setting appointments for sales reps – Cold calling is an expensive and frustrating way of making initial contact with prospects. Sometimes it makes more sense to use telemarketers to phone ahead to schedule appointments for sales reps.

7. Following up other media – Campaigns using telemar-

keting to follow up other marketing activities achieve substantially better results than campaigns using only one medium.

8. Pre-qualifying leads – Leads generated from most sources can range from worthless to extremely valuable. If you turn leads over to sales personnel without pre-qualification, sales reps may ignore most or all of the leads. However, if you qualify your leads by telephone before giving them to the sales force, and pass on only those that are qualified, you can achieve a significant improvement in the closing percentage.

9. Testing new lists – You can use telemarketing to test outside mailing lists before their use in other media.

10. Researching the market – The telephone is a good marketing research tool, especially if you have a list that is unresponsive to online surveys. You can utilize telemarketing to pre-test new products, services, offers, benefits, and market areas.

Telemarketing has several advantages that recommend its use as an important part of the marketing mix:

*   Telemarketing can work – Organizations that use telemarketing once (assuming it is implemented properly) tend to continue its use.

*   Telemarketing is measurable – As with other direct response methods, it is easy to determine an exact cost-per-inquiry, cost-per-lead, and cost-per-sale. With this information, you not only know where you stand on

the current project, you also receive a steady stream of response data that helps improve future programs.

- Telemarketing is fast – All you need to get started with telemarketing is a telephone, someone to make the calls, and a list of people to call. You can follow email programs with telephone calls to create integrated media campaigns and complete the entire cycle in a couple of weeks.

- Telemarketing is flexible – Telemarketing expenses are primarily based on equipment and personnel costs. Once a program begins, you can modify the product, offer, and script at any time, with little or no increase in cost.

- Telemarketing can be cost-effective – While it is not cheap, a telemarketing contact costs only a small fraction of the average cost of a personal sales call. Granted, a larger percentage of person-to-person calls will result in a sale; but in terms of cost-effectiveness, telephone selling can prove to be a much better investment.

The telephone does have its drawbacks as a marketing and selling tool. For one thing, telemarketing is an intrusive medium. Every other promotional activity gives the prospect some degree of control, but he or she has no choice as to the timing of your telephone sales call. Outbound calling is a push marketing technique that can annoy people who prefer pull methods. Many business people react negatively to telephone calls and good portions of them never answer their phones just to avoid solicitors (myself included). In addition, although you can generate leads for complex offers, it is difficult to sell expensive and/or complex products via the phone (difficult, but not impossible).

Telemarketing can work by itself, but not as well as when combined with other marketing tools such as email and direct mail. I tested this recently with a white paper offer, using the same database for all three list splits.

> List 1 – 5,000 contacts emailed with no follow-up: 41 responses = .8% response rate
>
> List 2 – 5,000 contacts called with no prior email: 74 responses = 1.5% response rate
>
> List 3 – 5,000 contacts emailed with phone follow-up: 122 responses = 2.4% response rate

The results were conclusive with the integrated campaign generating more response than the two single-shot programs put together.

How to Make Your Telephone Calls Count

Most telephone sales reps use a prepared script. The script can be as basic as an outline of key selling points, or it can be an exact listing of the words you want the telephone sales rep (TSR) to say, including her response to objections and questions. Generally, the more experienced the TSR, the less reliance on a detailed script is necessary. My advice is to make the script as detailed as possible, but give your TSRs maximum leeway to change the wording to fit their unique personalities.

One important point—find out what your competitors are doing and take a different approach. Having been the recipient of hundreds of B2B solicitation calls over the years (which seem like thousands), I get very annoyed when multiple companies call me using essentially the same script. If you are practicing the Fusion Marketing principles of positioning shared in this book, you will not have a "me, too" company. Express your unique selling proposition in a provocative and compelling way that differentiates your company from its competitors. That is the way to cut through the clutter and get noticed.

Always remember the context in which the telephone call is made. You are likely disrupting some activity, since few people are sitting by their telephones hoping to receive a sales call. Therefore, you must grab the prospect's attention immediately and open with a compelling benefit. In other words, *get to the point quickly*. Do not open a conversation by asking the prospect how he is doing or about the weather at his location. Instead of serving as effective icebreakers, these questions merely irritate the caller and tell him you have little respect for his time. In a similar vein, do not become overly familiar with the prospect.

Introduce yourself and your company immediately. Do not leave the prospect in suspense about who you are. The prospect cannot concentrate on what you are saying until his curiosity about who you are is satisfied. State the purpose of your call – "I am following up on information I sent you about ABC last week." Then lead with your biggest benefit by quickly telling your prospect how he will profit from your product or service. Then continue with secondary benefits. If your prospect doesn't show positive response to benefit number one, continue sharing benefits until you hit the person's hot button.

Train your TSRs to be pleasantly persistent but never curt, rude, or overly aggressive. If they must use pressure, teach them Mark Twain's definition of tact: "Tact is the ability to tell a man to go to hell, and make him glad to be on his way."

So far, we have been referring to outbound telephone selling, where a representative takes the initiative by placing a call to the prospect. In contrast, with inbound telemarketing, the prospect places a call to your organization, usually in response to an online, print, direct mail, or broadcast ad featuring a toll-free number. You can use inbound telemarketing for direct sales or lead generation, running the gamut from simply answering a call and taking an order, to the beginning of a complex selling process. Just as with outbound telephone selling, you may want to consider a professional service bureau to handle your inbound needs.

One key to a successful inbound telephone operation is to gather as much information as possible from each prospect who calls. If you sell directly, this data will make your in-house customer file much more valuable, and if you are capturing leads, the extra information will increase the likelihood of converting these leads into sales. Asking the questions will often help the qualification process, since a prospect who is reluctant to provide your operators with information is probably not a very good candidate for your product or service.

In-House or Service Bureau

When you decide to begin a telemarketing program, you will have to answer a very important question: whether to manage and implement your program in-house, or hire an outside service bureau to do it for you. You should base this decision on a number of factors including the complexity of your product or service; the number of inbound and/ or outbound calls expected; availability of trained management and telephone reps; in-house expertise in telemarketing; amount of dollars allocated to the project; physical space restrictions; and length of the telemarketing campaign.

Generally, the following are circumstances where you might want to utilize an outside service bureau:

- When you need to get started right away. A good service bureau can have your program underway much faster than you can allocate necessary resources to the project.

- When you don't have the initial investment needed for equipment, space, and personnel. Telemarketing start-up costs are high. A service bureau charges only for the specific services provided, although you and other clients will also pay an amortized portion of the company's equipment, space, and personnel costs.

- When the flow of incoming and outgoing calls fluctuates. As an employer, you need to provide your TSRs with some degree of job security. On the other hand, you certainly do not want to pay people to stare at telephones that are not ringing, or to pay people who do not have anyone to call. A service bureau solves this problem because they charge you only for the time its personnel are making (or receiving) calls on your behalf.

- When the campaign is of short duration. If you plan to make an ongoing commitment to the telemarketing medium, consider an in-house program. Otherwise, work with a service bureau.

- When you lack the necessary expertise. Service bureaus are paid to provide telemarketing services. This is not a game for the fainthearted or inexperienced, and if you are unwilling to make the commitment to the training that this medium requires, use a service bureau.

Here are reasons to consider bringing your telemarketing program in-house:

- Saving money. Unless your program is completely inefficient, you should be able to run an in-house program at much less cost than using an outside service bureau.

- Faster feedback. Your in-house personnel will be able to react very rapidly to any changes in the market since they are receiving up-to-the-minute feedback from prospects.

- Close coordination with other marketing activities. If you manage your print advertising, direct mail, and other activities in-house, it may be a good idea to also handle the telemarketing program this way.

- Exercising greater control over the program. No matter how flexible an outside service bureau is, you lose some degree of control by delegating the program. Hands-on means maximum control.

If telephoning is an important part of your marketing plans, then I highly recommend two experts who have assisted me in the past:

Michael A. Brown, Business to Business by Phone - www.michaelabrown.net - 800-373-3966

Kraig Kleeman – Blaire Group - www.blairegroup.com – 800-654-7887

Success Tip: When in doubt, use a professional telemarketing service and bring the program in-house later.

Part VI

The People Element — How to Build and Motivate Your Team

Chapter 29

Cultivate a Healthy
Marketing Environment

---

*"I look on that man as happy, who, when there is a
question of success, looks into his work for a reply."*
— Ralph Waldo Emerson

There is a tendency in marketing and sales to do whatever it takes to get attention and make the sale, regardless of the long-term effect. This has created a harsh climate, where it is legitimate to offend a small portion of the audience as long as enough people buy. The worst offenders in my opinion are advertisements that insult any single group of people, such as business people, women, minorities, ethnic groups, or the physically or mentally disabled; ads that use sex to get attention when it has nothing to do with the product; ads that encourage or glorify violence; or ads that denigrate any religion or religious practice.

Surprisingly, agencies and copywriters who come up with such offensive ideas (usually based on clichés we were all exposed to in grammar school) believe that they are being creative, in the same way that television sitcom writers claim to be funny by inserting tired and trite dialogue, designed to elicit snickers instead of genuine laughter, into their programs. George Gilder, writing in *Life After Television*, referred to this as "formulaic banality," and sadly, it is no less a factor in marketing promotions than in television.

Unfortunately, entire industries can be negatively influenced by the actions of the bad actors. So do yourself a favor. Do not be a bad actor and resort to the easy, the cheap, or the crude. Instead, market in such a manner that you help improve the business climate.

Likewise, two of the most important virtues you should strive for in your marketing and sales are integrity and congruence. Congruent marketing means that the message you communicate should always match the reality of what the customer can expect at the point-of-service. Inconsistent promotional themes often cause incongruence, since the people who see the message have no idea of the true character of the advertiser.

Unfortunately, examples of incongruent advertising are all too available. When a bank advertises that "long lines are a thing of the past," and people go to that bank and wait in a long line, that's incongruent. When a company promises a full-satisfaction guarantee, and the customer almost has to beg to get his money back, that's incongruent. Customers will never forgive you if you betray their faith, so you are far better off leaving inaccurate messages out of your copy. This is not just a moral imperative, but a practical one as well. Social media helps people vent their displeasure and if you do not treat people with integrity and congruence, they have the means to tell many others. This is why airlines are now monitoring Twitter traffic – so that they can head off problems while the disgruntled passenger is still at the airport.

Focus on Strengths

Another way to create a positive environment is to focus on your strengths, and those of your staff, instead of weaknesses. This may seem counterintuitive, but trust me, you will be far more successful in a job that makes use of what you like to do and at what you happen to excel. And it's funny how often these two things are the same. What you like to do, you are good at, and what you hate to do, is not in your core area of competence. My advice is to embrace and not fight this fact. We have all had bosses who tried to improve us by ignoring our strengths and focusing on our weaknesses. To paraphrase a boss from many years ago, "Chris, you're a strong strategic marketer, leader and communicator, but you need to spend time learning about graphic design and how to produce comprehensive Excel spreadsheets. Also, you are not especially detail-oriented so work on that as well."

What I should have replied at the time, but didn't, is the fact that I had people in my department who were great at graphic design, spreadsheets, and managing projects. I was producing impressive results using my natural talents and well-honed skills and these results were far too important to the company than any benefits gained by my struggle to develop minimal skills in areas that were not interesting to me. So if you have such a boss, share these reasons to let you concentrate on what you do best:

1. What you excel at tends to be much easier for you. In fact, it can seem so natural and effortless that you take your accomplishments for granted and minimize the particular skill. But from a time and energy perspective, this is where you will provide the most value at the least cost.

2. Time spent on your areas of weakness will at best get you to a fair or mediocre skill set. Remember when Michael Jordan decided to become a baseball player and decided to neglect his core skill (basketball). The world's greatest basketball player was, at best, average

in another sport. If you are a Michael Jordan at something, stick with what you are good at.

3. People who are forced to act in areas that are not natural are stressed and unhappy, while focusing on their core competencies makes them happier—and happier workers tend to be workers that are more productive.

4. The people you hire to backfill your areas of weakness will also be happier and more productive, because they are concentrating on their strengths. This is much more beneficial to you and to the company.

If these four reasons are not enough to convince the skeptical boss to let you focus on your areas of strength, then remind him or her of what management guru Peter Drucker said: "Your strengths will carry you through to success." What is good for you is good for the staff you manage, so also make it a point to discover and nurture their strengths.

Success Tip: To create a healthy environment, focus on what your staff is good at, and make sure all your promotional messages reflect integrity and congruence.

Chapter 30

Assemble an Unbeatable Marketing Team

*"Work is a privilege. It's a privilege to be able to do
what you love to do and be good at it. My hobby is
my work, and my work is my hobby. That's the secret.
There's no distinction."*

– Les Paul, guitar legend

This chapter could be the most important you read, because in the ultra-serious business of going to war against your competitors, the members of your marketing team will prove to be either your most important asset, or your worst nightmare. I am going to discuss how to find, hire, train, and motivate an outstanding team without breaking your budget. Suffice it to say that if you are either the head of the marketing department or a line manager, hiring and supervising people will prove to be a serious challenge or a fun and productive endeavor—and sometimes both of these things in the same week.

Characteristics of the Highly Effective Marketing Team

Leo Tolstoy wrote in *Anna Karenina*, "Happy families are all alike; every unhappy family is unhappy in its own way." This is equally true for marketing departments. Part of the successful team is due to chemistry, some to careful selection, and some to good old-fashioned luck and timing, but in my experience, great teams do share five common characteristics:

1.   They are results-driven and dedicated to success. They want to know how they are measured and feel pride when they meet their objectives and disappointment when they do not. They take winning and losing seriously and they know how the mission of the marketing department relates to and supports the entire organization.

2.   They are totally responsible for their unique objectives. Just as the team has it goals, so too do the individual members of the team. The person who writes copy is dependent on the media buyer, and if the ad or promotion isn't run in the right media, the results will be poor. The lead qualification team depends on the outbound lead generation specialist to provide sources of inquires to be qualified. There are dozens of such interdependencies in the average marketing department and if any member of the team is weak, it impacts the entire team.

3.   They have fun. Let's face it—there are people out there who are so sour they might as well have been weaned on dill pickles. They are not the type of people I want to spend time with, on or off duty. Although good teammates take the mission seriously and watch the scorecard, they don't take themselves too seriously. After all, we are not finding the cure for cancer, or saving anyone's life; we are simply practicing the art of marketing and sales. Just as in sports, a loose mar-

keting and sales team usually performs better than an uptight team. A little laughter can be a powerful boost to the hardworking marketing team, in good times and tough times.

4. They like and respect each other. It is a painful experience to work around people who don't like each other. Chemistry will take you far when times are rough. The team doesn't have to go drinking together every night but it helps if they have a genuine fondness for each other. Equally important is the fact that each member of the team has respect for the professional capabilities of the other members.

5. They are dedicated to learning. It is hard to improve if you are not learning. Marketing is a profession that changes constantly and it is important to keep up with the newest techniques, media, technology, etc.

How to Find and Motivate Good Marketers

Networking is by far the best source of talented marketers. I have found great teammates by emailing to friends and by using social media services such as LinkedIn. Craigslist is becoming popular as a low cost way of finding employees. However, regardless of where I find candidates, I always prefer to talk to one or more people who have worked with the candidate, but are not on the official reference list. These unofficial *back-door references* tend to be much more accurate.

Sometimes you will hear someone say they want all "A" players on the team and will only settle for the best talent. However, this is often a mistake. Depending on the work to be done, reporting relationships, etc., it might be a good idea to have a mixture of A's, B's and perhaps even a C or two. Superstars are hard to find, are much more expensive, and don't always play well together. For you baseball fans, witness the recent saga of the New York Yankees, who do not win the big prize every year despite the marquee lineup and huge payroll. They are often beaten by teams with fewer superstars, but know how to play well together.

Team chemistry can be as important as individual talent, so make sure that the existing staff has a lot to say about who is hired. Peer pressure can be a strong positive force but can become unbalanced when new people join the team without proper vetting. If existing employees feel they had a part in the hiring process, their motivation to help the new employees become successful will be much stronger. I have used the team hiring strategy many times, and it has never failed.

Remember the four C's to create and maintain a successful team environment:

Caring manager

Competency expected in the work environment

Camaraderie among the troops

Compensation system that rewards individual and team performance

What to Do When Someone Isn't Working Out

To be honest, I have always wrestled with the question of what to do with underperformers. Having made every mistake in the book while hiring and managing hundreds of marketing and sales personnel over the past two decades, I have come to the conclusion that it is better to find good people in the first place than it is to train people to be good. Some people have the desire and ability to change and some improve with coaching, but for the most part, if they start their career with you as a good employee, this is what they will remain. This is why you should heed the admonition to always "hire slowly and fire quickly." If you do this, firing anyone will be a rare event.

It is important to let people know exactly what you expect of them, hopefully in measurable terms. You would be surprised at how many employees have no idea of their boss' expectations. While the issue of whether employees are conscientious or have a cooperative attitude is subjective, the question of whether they met their lead generation goal is not subjective. It is much easier to have a conversation about what isn't working if you have some facts on which to base your assessment.

When you sense that a member of your marketing or sales team is going off track, it is better to address this quickly than to let it linger. Newton's law of inertia states, "An object at rest tends to stay at rest, and an object in motion tends to stay in motion with the same speed and in the same direction unless acted upon by an unbalanced force." This is also true for humans, and as a manager, one of your jobs is to change the direction of employee performance if it is not contributing to the success of the company and/or your department. Try to be encouraging when you do this. After all, if you did not believe in the competence of the employee, you would not have hired him or her. But also be very clear about what the employee must do to meet their obligations. After the initial talk, you should check for progress frequently.

Firing people is very painful, which is why it is better to hire slowly and carefully. However, if you must terminate an underperforming employee, try to do it as quickly and painlessly as possible. Usually, you will get no thanks for any coaching that you do during the termination process, if that coaching is about how the employee should overcome some particular weakness. By the time it gets to the point where you feel the need to sever a relationship, the employee may dislike you and/or distrust you, and will take any constructive criticism as a hostile act. Even worse, he or she may use your words against you. To reduce the possibility of this happening, you are usually better off eliminating someone's position instead of terminating for cause. If you take this route, do not mix the elimination of the position with a discussion of the employee's shortcomings. You can simply say, "We are eliminating your position and this has nothing to do with your performance." Isn't that much easier?

The Most Important Attribute of a Good Marketer

After a recent presentation, someone asked me, "Chris, what do you consider the most important attribute of a good marketer?" Without hesitation, I said, "Someone who accepts the monkey." I am not sure where I first learned about the concept, but the idea is that tasks, projects, responsibilities, etc., are like monkeys. Until a particular item is finished, it is like a monkey on your back that you have to feed, think about, and so on. In other words, you are responsible for that monkey.

Regardless of your title, you always have one or more monkeys to worry about, and the higher you go in the food chain, the more monkeys there are that command your attention. If you have an uninterested or incompetent staff, you will need to worry about every monkey. However, if you have a competent and enthusiastic staff, they will gladly accept many of the monkeys and free you from worrying about every project and every detail.

Therefore, the moral of the story is: Do not monkey around. Find great people to staff your team, motivate them well, and sleep soundly.

Tips for Managing Your Staff

Here are some additional ideas for running a happy and productive marketing operation:

- Do not micromanage. It's not fun for you or your employee. If you micromanage because you cannot help it, work on yourself. If you micromanage because your employee is incompetent, replace the employee.

- Do not expect perfection. As Keith Cunningham said, "Don't let perfection interfere with possible."

- Focus on what really matters: *results*, not meetings, hours, or report. There is an intriguing concept in management theory called ROWE, which stands for Results-Only Work Environment. Check this out.

- Reward risk-taking. You need to let your staff know that it is okay to make mistakes, as long as they learn from those mistakes.

- Welcome diversity. If you are following the suggestions in this chapter and the rest of the book, you will not care whether the members of your team are white, yellow, black, or brown. Nor will you care whether they are young or old, male or female, straight or gay, conservative or liberal. Diversity of backgrounds, thoughts, and ideas can be a positive force for progress. So resist the temptation to only hire people in your own image. However, there is one caveat: I prefer not to hire anyone who is not talented, fun, and results-driven. Diversity is not a good idea when it comes to these attributes.

- Caring produces positive results, but don't let your people get too close.

- Be the leader. The work environment is not a democracy.

- Remember the words of Herbert Kelleher, founder of Southwest Airlines: "Your people come first, and if you treat them right, they'll treat customers right, and the customers will come back, and that'll make the shareholders happy." It cannot be said any better than this.

Success Tip: Treat the hiring and motivation of a good team as your most important task.

Chapter 31

Hire and Grow Top Sales Performers

"If you pick the right people and give them the opportunity to spread their wings—and put compensation as a carrier behind it—you almost don't have to manage them."

— Jack Welch

Jack Welch, former CEO of GE, has it right. Picking the right people, giving them independence, and backing them up with a good compensation plan can have enormous rewards. People who manage sales departments would find their jobs a lot easier and more productive if they would adopt this philosophy.

The goal of any sales organization should be to maximize output in the most efficient manner possible. In other words, you want to reap the most revenue while putting out the least amount of effort. This is true for everyone in the department, including the sales manager or sales VP. And it is doubly true if you have to manage the sales department along with other aspects of the business. However, you may be one of those people who have created incompatibility between the characteristics of the sales team and your management style. If this is the case, your team is probably frustrated, you are frustrated, and no one is as effective as they should be.

Start by asking yourself a crucial question: Do you prefer to hire relatively inexperienced sales reps, and train them in your way of selling? Alternatively, do you prefer to hire experienced reps who already know how to sell? The answer to this question will drive a fundamental decision about how you should run your sales operation. If you hire inexperienced reps, you will need to devote a great deal of time to training and monitoring your personnel. On the other hand, if your hiring plan calls for experienced sales personnel, they will (should) require much less hands-on training and monitoring.

Here are three scenarios where your hiring and management style can produce *negative* results:

1. If you hire rookies and expect them to perform like veterans, without a great deal of help, you will be disappointed by their performance.

2. If you hire veterans and treat them like rookies, you will increase your workload, increase their frustration, and decrease your results.

3. If you hire a mixed team of veterans and rookies, you will have to adjust your management style or end up with frustration, poor results, or both.

One of my consulting clients had a VP of sales that was a typical Type A personality. This guy liked to hire solid veteran sales reps—the type of people that were used to big deals and achieving million dollar quotas. This was fine but he then proceeded to treat the sales dream team like a bunch of minor leaguers. He told them how to prospect and he told them how to close sales. He put the veteran reps in a cold-call class that was designed for junior lead qualification personnel. Worse, he constantly criticized the actions that had served these sales reps so well in the past. Naturally, the veterans were frustrated, lost confidence in their boss, and failed to make their quotas.

On the other end of the scale, you have the situation where rookies are thrown into the sales fray with little instruction and little mentoring, yet they are expected to start producing like veterans. There are some reps who can survive in this type of environment, but most will fail. New sales reps have many advantages: they are less expensive and have not developed bad habits—but they do require more handholding. Follow this plan if you have the time, patience, and training materials necessary to give these people a solid underpinning in both your product or service and sales process. However, if you do not have the time and tools to mentor new reps, choose a different path.

If you choose to go the veteran route, the best thing you can do is find out what they believe they need to be successful and give it to them. Please re-read the preceding sentence. Give people what they believe *they need* to be successful, not what you think they need. Your role becomes that of a mentor and coach, not a director or micro-manager. Carry the attitude of "How can I help you meet your sales objectives?" This posture of service will gain you support and loyalty and you will not have to work as hard to get positive results.

In this model, you are placing a lot of trust in your team and supporting them fully. You may have guidelines, but you are willing to interpret these guidelines generously and give your reps more slack than normally makes you feel comfortable. However, only do this if you have hired self-directed and responsible people who have a record of delivering results. And in return for your trust and support, you can expect these reps to take greater ownership of their goals and how they achieve these goals. I prefer that sales reps think of themselves not so much as employees but almost as franchisees or distributors. Their territory becomes their business and the monkey is on their backs to ensure the business is successful.

Like everything else, this issue is not entirely black or white. You can often find good performers that fall in the middle, not quite rookies but not yet established veterans. These people will require a bit more support, but the sooner you can get them into a self-sufficiency mindset, the better. And even veterans can use ongoing training, both in your product or service and to keep their sales skills sharp. The trick is to match your hiring plan with your management style, so that you have a team in place that is congruent with your preferred operational model.

Success Tip: Hire right and manage less and you can work less and achieve more.

Chapter 32

Motivate for Outstanding Sales Results

"Motivation is everything. You can do the work of two people, but you can't be two people. Instead you have to inspire the next guy down the line and get him to inspire his people."

– Lee Iacocca

Assuming that you have a good team of sales professionals, you obviously want them to become a great team. There are many ways to do this, but basically, you can motivate by reward (carrot) or by punishment (stick). Interestingly, about half the population is primarily motivated by carrots and the other half by sticks. Of course, many of us are driven by multiple styles, but I am speaking about primary motivations.

One way to determine if you are the carrot or stick manager is to watch the movie *Glengarry Glen Ross*. If you identify with the sales manager character played by Alec Baldwin, you are definitely a stick manager, especially if you identify with his famous line: "Get away from the coffee. Coffee is for closers." If you have not seen this film, it is definitely worthwhile. I personally find the Alec Baldwin character offensive and would not want to work for or around such a person, but there are those who feel it is a legitimate management style.

I have directly managed many salespeople over the years and as a senior marketing executive have closely observed the management style of dozens of B2B sales managers, in companies ranging from start-ups to billion dollar organizations. The very best sales teams have been reward-based and not punishment-based. Such teams and such managers simply produce better.

I prefer the reward-based motivation for another reason. Business is tough enough as it is, and it's hard to keep your own attitude positive if you are forced to beat people up to get them to perform. So the carrot environment is certainly preferable to the stick environment. Plus, in the reward-based environment, you are often trying to get people to succeed in a big way, to exceed quota, to close the bigger deals. Conversely, in the punishment-based environment, you are often whipping and threatening people just to maintain a minimal level of performance, and this can be as draining on you as it is on your people.

In some ways, it is inaccurate to say that we motivate performance in others. Rather, we help enable the factors that already motivate them. Some respond to the threat of being fired or going hungry (stick) while others work hard for the peer recognition, the money, or to please their manager (carrot).

Peer pressure is one of the strongest motivating forces. Several years ago I was VP of marketing for a large software company, and I was able to create an exceptional sales development team in a short period of time. Basically, we first hired a strong, empathetic manager who had been a sales development rep himself. We then hired two reps who the manager knew from a prior company. These two were given three months to prove themselves and establish a baseline performance benchmark. Since sales development reps qualify inbound inquiries, their production ramp is much quicker than field sales personnel who have to go through the long business-to-business sales cycle.

The three people in the department (manager plus two reps) were then given the task of hiring new sales development personnel. The three became four, five, six, and finally seven. My role as VP was to endorse the candidates selected by the manager and reps. Each new rep was told, in no uncertain terms, that he or she was responsible to start achieving the same production numbers as the experienced reps within one quarter. Everyone's compensation was based not only on individual performance but also on group performance, with some nice bonuses for significant upside performance.

I have rarely seen a group with more camaraderie and esprit de corps. Not only did the entire team stay together for several years, they made their qualified lead objectives for thirteen straight quarters, including six that fell in a bad economy. And as the responsible executive, I was fortunate to have not only a good line manager, but also a team that would police itself and motivate their peers. I have experienced situations like this several times in my career and have learned to appreciate each one greatly. This is another example of Fusion Marketing at its finest.

Bad Managers – Don't Be One

I have worked with many characters over the years, which is not a problem because I really like and appreciate unusual and interesting people. This is probably true for you as well. Unfortunately, a few of these people were less-than-stellar human beings and a couple had serious character flaws. One sales VP was such a rotten person on the job that I had almost a physical revulsion to him.

You may think I was overreacting to this guy, but he was indeed a pompous jerk. He once came into my office, sat down, and proceeded to clip his fingernails. (At least he sat next to the wastebasket). This was a classic power move—he was trying to show that he was in a superior position as compared to yours truly. However, I had an unexpected reaction: I laughed. Even worse than his rudeness—he was a bully to his staff. I have always had a dislike of those who prey on weaker people—be that the street tough or the bully at work.

Let's face it—life is problematic enough without dealing with difficult people all day. We may not have a choice of our coworkers and other aspects of our work environment. However, we do have a choice of how we respond to and treat others. Frankly, we would all be better off if the would-be office tyrants and dictators were confronted more often.

Here are five other characteristics of bad bosses, as reported by *CFO Finance Daily*:

1.   Bad bosses blame others.

2.   Bad bosses drag their feet.

3.   Bad bosses can't be trusted.

4.   Bad bosses get (and accept) a free pass.

5.   Bad bosses are credit hogs.

It is a good idea for you (and me) to take a hard look at your management style to make sure you are not exhibiting these characteristics. If you feel the need to be a hard-nose type of boss, perhaps it is because you believe that nice guys finish last. If you are nice, people will take advantage, they will dump extra work on you, they will push you around, etc. This is especially pernicious in sales, where some people assume that you have to be a take-no-prisoners bulldog to make quota. The theory goes that marketing people can afford to be nicer since they aren't trying to pick the pockets of customers.

Being a nice person is not synonymous with being a doormat. There are many ways being a decent person can reap dividends. People will help you because you have a title or because you can influence their career. However, if you are a jerk, people will find ways to withhold support if you lose the title or influence. They may even quit returning your phone calls. Remember the expression: Be careful how you treat people on the way up because you may see them on your way down. So if you are a genuinely good person, you will not lack for support on either the way up or way down. Common decency is always good for fostering workplace camaraderie and cooperation.

To see how these platitudes pan out in real life, try a little experiment. List every boss you can remember and label them as nice, neutral, or mean. Also label them as highly successful, moderately successful, or unsuccessful. Now see if there is any correlation between being a nice or mean boss and success. In my case, I was able to assign ratings to fourteen previous bosses. In my subjective opinion, three of these individuals were mean, seven nice, and four neutral. And while I am not privy to the personal finances of all of these people, my best guess is that four are what I would call highly successful: two from the nice group, one from the mean group, and one from the neutral group.

I would like to report that all the nice execs were highly successful and the mean execs were living on bread and water. However, it appears that successful people come from the same pool as the rest of us, with our mixes of character, assets, and liabilities. Since there is no liability in being nice, let us all do our coworkers and ourselves a favor and make the workplace a more humane and decent place. Heck, we may even get rich in the process.

Remember, I am not suggesting that you be a pushover. However, even if you believe in crushing your opponent, remember that crushing your internal staff is not the same thing. The war is out there in the marketplace, not in the office, and especially not against your own teammates.

If the foregoing is not enough to convince you to be a nice person at the office, think about this: Do you really want someone at your funeral saying, "That (*insert your name*) was a rotten human being but he sure was good at his job"?

Success Tip: *Do not work for a bad manager and don't be one your-self.*

Part VII

Taking it to the Next Level – Advanced Marketing and Sales Strategies

Chapter 33

Accelerate Your Business with Viral Marketing

"If the Internet can be described as a giant human consciousness, then viral marketing is the illusion of free will."

– George Pendle

The good news is that viral marketing is a Fusion Marketing strategy that can help you grow your business tremendously. The not-so-good news is that it is quite hard to make viral marketing work effectively. You need to have a combination of impeccable execution, luck, and timing. Many companies have tried viral marketing and only a few have succeeded in a big way. However, even those that are not big winners can often create positive outcomes. Therefore, you have everything to gain and nothing to lose by trying viral marketing.

If the words *viral marketing* conjure up images of diseases or computer bugs, there is good reason. According to Wikipedia, "The buzzwords viral marketing and viral advertising refer to marketing techniques that use pre-existing social networks to produce increases in brand awareness or to achieve other marketing objectives (such as product sales) through self-replicating viral processes, analogous to the spread of pathological and computer viruses." In his book *Media Virus,* Douglas Rushkoff used the disease analogy as follows: The assumption is that if such an advertisement reaches a "susceptible" user, that user will become "infected" (i.e., accept the idea) and will then go on to share the idea with others, "infecting them," in the viral analogy's terms.

Viral marketing campaigns share the following six characteristics:

1. They are self-perpetuating.

2. They are timely and relevant.

3. They allow for easy forwarding of the message.

4. They have messages that are clear and intuitive.

5. They are interactive.

6. They can quickly scale from small to large campaigns.

Viral Marketing Strategies

One of the great things about viral marketing is that its results can be exponential, not linear. For example, direct marketing can be somewhat predictable based on response statistics—you know that adding X amount of dollars in marketing expenses generates Y dollars in revenue. However, putting the same amount of dollars into a viral marketing campaign could generate Y dollars, YY dollars, or YYY dollars. It is a beautiful thing when you can make it happen, and this is why viral marketing is a strategy that can accelerate your business success. Here are some ideas of how you can make it happen for your company.

1. Give something away. People love to get free stuff and giveaways are a great way to build attention and loyalty.

Information is a particularly good giveaway because it is inexpensive to distribute (especially electronically) and can easily be segmented. In other words, you can give away a taste of information to draw respondents into your orbit. Articles and e-books are great giveaways, as well as research surveys and third-party reports.

2. Create something amazing. Unless you are a large company, it can be tough to generate attention. Therefore, you need to be unique. You can do this by entertaining or provoking (or both). Funny works. Big statements work. Challenging the conventional wisdom works. But never do anything that creates so much controversy that it weakens your brand. And don't be too clever for your own good by launching a campaign that is great at drawing attention to the creative gimmick, but lousy at reinforcing your company brand. In other words, the campaign must be relevant to the prospect and to what it is that you offer.

3. Make it a series. You are not always going to hit a home run on a campaign. Sometimes it is better to create a series of information pieces or promotions that reinforce the message and build an audience over time.

4. Be persistent. To continue the baseball analogy, the only way to hit home runs is to swing hard—which also increases your chance of striking out. The same is true in marketing. You have to try things that may or may not work. Unless you have a better crystal ball than I do, you must be willing to accept the risk of failed campaigns, the marketing equivalent of striking out.

5. Use the right media vehicles to propagate your message. The right media vehicle is the one that will get the right people to respond. The hottest viral marketing campaigns seem to land on YouTube but B2B marketers can have great success using the press, blogosphere, LinkedIn, Twitter, etc.

6. Reinforce what you are doing in viral marketing with traditional media. You can do this by providing links in your emails, advertisements, corporate Website, etc. You can also incorporate the viral marketing campaign into your public relations activities.

7. Capture contact information. Generating attention is nice, but what really accelerates your success in B2B marketing is building a database of prospects, customers, and followers that you can nurture over time and sell to repeatedly. Every viral or non-viral marketing activity should help build your database.

8. Have a follow-up strategy. Remember what they say about the dog that chases the bus: What does he do when he catches it? The same is true in viral marketing. Prepare for whatever level of attention you get. Have a specific lead-nurturing strategy including pre-planned auto-responses to immediately communicate with those who download or request your materials. Use a strong offer to convert these responders into first-time customers. Think carefully about how you will use the results of the campaign to create solid prospects and revenue.

9. Publicize your success. This is the fun part. Suppose you have created a buzz about your campaign and

your company and exceeded all your campaign objectives. Do not stop there. Alert the press and use the social media outlets to let the world know about your campaign. Some of the most successful campaigns received more attention after the fact than they did while they were running. This add-on publicity can turn a warm effort into a red-hot publicity machine.

An example of a creative, fun and successful viral marketing campaign was one of the winners of last year's Marketing Sherpa Viral Hall of Fame. As related at the MarketingSherpa site: "This Northwestern Mutual Insurance campaign encouraged microsite visitors to 'let it go.' Visitors to the interactive page could select concerns, such as financial troubles or illness, and dispose of them via catapult, rocket, submarine, or hot air balloon. The microsite leveraged a tell-a-friend feature and could be shared on social media sites, such as Digg and Del.icio.us. By the third month of the campaign, the site's traffic was 213% higher than Northwestern Mutual's total microsite traffic for the previous year." You can read more about this campaign and other viral marketing award winners at marketingsherpa.com/viralawards.

Another excellent resource is David Meerman Scott's book, *The New Rules of Viral Marketing*, available for free download at davidmeermanscott.com/documents/Viral_Marketing.pdf. In the quick-read book, Scott explains how he went from a relative unknown to 100,000 references on Google in a very short time, through the power of viral marketing.

Success Tip: Try viral marketing because it can take your marketing and sales to new heights.

Chapter 34

Add Value to Products and Services

"The key to creating wealth is simple. It is called adding value. Successful people are those who are always looking for ways to add value in some way to a person, a company, a product or a service."

– Brian Tracy

Although many marketers refuse to believe this, widespread access to technical advancements in most industries has led to a "death of the product solution." This is especially true in the high-technology marketplace. But the truth is, since so many products are similar in quality and functionality, the secret is not to differentiate what your product is, but rather to differentiate what it can do for the prospect. This is, after all, the only thing that really concerns the buyer. In this world of commodity products, you must find a way to set yourself apart. And it is not only substance that will set you apart, it is also style.

One of the best examples of the importance of style is the clothing industry. Do you ever wonder why one pair of jeans sells for two to three times the price of another, or why a pair of in-style tennis shoes sells for four times the price of the run-of-the-mill brand? I challenge the average consumer to explain what it is that makes the expensive shoe so valuable. It is, in fact, a commodity product that has been differentiated.

You can also differentiate services with added value. Anything that differentiates you from the competition can be considered value-add. For example, if you are a public speaker, you can give everyone a copy of your latest book, DVD, or research report. Or you could give audience members a free ticket to another one of your presentations. In fact, the list of things you can do is long. Just choose one or more that costs you little while gaining lots of appreciation from your customers.

Here are some additional ideas of how you can add value to your existing products or services:

1. Enhance the product or service with technical improvements. As noted above, this strategy has limitations because competitors will often counter with their own improvements.

2. Offer add-on services with your products. For instance, an automobile dealer can offer lifetime oil changes with the purchase of a new car, or a software supplier can offer free upgrades or a 24-hour assistance hotline.

3. Provide your customers with up-to-date or pre-packaged information about their industries and job functions. Everyone can use information that will make his or her job easier and more productive.

4. Provide a quick-start guide that helps your customers get started rapidly. If you do this, make sure the quick-start program works as advertised.

5. Offer expanded satisfaction guarantees and extended warranties. In fact, do anything you can to reduce the anxiety and fear the prospect has of making a bad decision.

6. Provide your customers with access to a unique or special

part of the Website that contains information that is not available to others.

7. Offer new delivery methods and/or shorten delivery times for your products. Waiting six to eight weeks for delivery is no longer acceptable, since Federal Express and UPS have trained customers to expect delivery within days.

8. Provide multimedia (audio, video, or Web) training that helps customers become proficient with your product or service.

9. Change the packaging or appearance of your product. Anything you can do to make it appear more exclusive or upscale will help support higher price points.

10. Find new uses for your product or service. Many technology companies have done this successfully by repackaging horizontal offerings as domain-specific or vertical offerings.

11. Deliver alliances with your product or service. This could come in the form of a strategic partnership or free membership in an industry association.

Be very careful about selecting a value-add that truly supports your unique selling proposition. It can be an expensive or even fatal mistake to focus on product enhancements that are of little interest to your prospects and customers. You will know that you have added value when your prospects either consistently purchase your product or service instead of the competition's, and/or they are willing to pay a premium price for what you offer.

Success Tip: To drive more revenue, find ways to enhance the value of your products and services.

Chapter 35

Make it Easy for People to Do Business with You

"We have met the enemy and he is us."

– Pogo by Walt Kelly

Please read this chapter carefully. And if you recognize anything you do that needs changing, be diligent about doing what is necessary to be a company that people find it easy to do business with. In other words, do nothing that prevents people from spending their money (or their company's money) with you. It is amazing how many ways organizations can find to put up the types of roadblocks that make it hard for people to locate research, engage, and purchase. You can get away with this if you are a government agency or monopoly, but most of us do not have that luxury.

Roadblocks can start early in the sales process with our awareness and lead generation programs. To sell someone anything, you must first educate them, so be generous about sharing information without prequalifying the prospect. Put yourself in the shoes of someone who is doing initial research. You want to learn enough to decide if you are truly interested, and when you are, you will be happy to engage with a salesperson—but not before.

Even though we are all consumers ourselves, why is this concept so tough to understand and embrace as marketers? It is because we face an ongoing battle to balance our desire to capture lead information against the equally important requirement to give prospects (or suspects) the information they need to learn more about what we offer without giving away their precious contact information. The devil on our left shoulder says, "Don't give away any information without capturing at least a name and email address." The angel on our right shoulder says, "Let's give away more of our information to make it easier for people to learn about us in a non-pressured way." As in most other aspects of life, you are probably wise to listen to the angel.

To get your ideas widespread attention, you have to give up on the idea of always capturing prospect data through Web forms, business reply cards, toll-free operators, etc. And although I am as hardcore of a direct marketer as they come, and am always looking to prove ROI on my campaigns, I believe most of us take this desire to collect information to an extreme. It may sound counterintuitive, but sometimes we gain more by giving up a little control. Of course we want to capture prospect information, but there are ways to do this without requiring registration on every contact.

The key is to balance the quality and value of what you are supplying with the type of data you are collecting from the prospect, so that he or she perceives it as a worthwhile trade. You are then creating a spirit of cooperation, rather than resentment. In the end, this philosophy can lead to greater amounts of revenue. It can also make your prospect comfortable in the early stages of your relationship. In fact, you will be rewarded for anything you do to let the prospect know that you are willing to share information without pressure. Of course, when it is time to close the deal, make sure you close the deal.

Take the following steps to determine if you are making it easy or tough for people to do business with you:

1. Give someone who is unaware of your company your marketing materials. Ask if they understand what you are selling, the benefits, terms, etc.

2. Go to your own Website, download the content, order the white paper, engage with the sales rep, monitor follow-up, purchase the product online (if you allow this), go through every step and see where it seems like a difficult process. Find the errors and trouble spots yourself, so your prospects won't have to.

3. Pick the thorniest and most unusual problem you can think of and see if you can easily find the answer at the customer support section of your Website.

4. Contact customer support (anonymously) via email and telephone to see if they can answer your questions, have the right attitude, and get back to you when promised.

5. Use your products yourself. It is amazing how often executives are shocked to discover how poorly their products actually work—because they have never had the user experience.

As a marketing or sales professional, you should also be learning directly from your customers. Jack Welch, the extraordinary former CEO of GE, spent up to 100 days a year speaking with customers. Likewise, Michael Dell, founder of Dell Computer, reportedly spends a great deal of time listening to customer support tapes of both happy and dissatisfied customers. If these great business leaders can find time to learn directly from customers, then you can do the same.

To share an example of how to make it hard to do business—I was recently looking for an online backup system for my home computer and went Web-surfing to find candidates. After reading online reviews, I decided to check out a particular company's Website. It seemed like a decent service for a reasonable price, but I had one important question: Could the service automatically backup desktop files as well as those I put in the "My Documents" folder? After hunting around their Website for ten minutes, I used the online chat feature to communicate with a customer service rep. Unfortunately, this individual could not answer my very simple question. However, she did promise to forward some documentation about how backup preferences are set, but not surprisingly, I never received the information.

What is the lesson to be learned from this experience? Simply this— it is better to make it easy for your prospects to find the information they are seeking, even if it does not frame you in a good light. If my simple question had been answered on the Website, I would not have had to deal with the customer support rep, nor she with me. In addition, I would not have been subjected to the disappointment of not receiving the promised information. The service was not expensive so the company did not lose much revenue on me. However, multiply my experience by many others and over time, it will affect their bottom line.

Your prospects are just as busy as you are. They want accurate information quickly. Give it to them and they will either buy from you or at the least, go away with a positive perception. Hide the information and they will leave with a negative impression, and perhaps write about you on their blog.

Success Tip: You must learn to view your company from the customer's point of view – what they see, hear, and experience when dealing with you.

Chapter 36

Rescue a Failing Marketing and Sales Operation

"Because a thing seems difficult for you, do not think it impossible for anyone to accomplish."

– Marcus Aurelius

If you spend some time in marketing or sales, you will probably face the challenge of rescuing a failing operation. Perhaps you are now in such a situation and despite the difficulties, you can probably relate to what Winston Churchill said: "Nothing in life is so exhilarating as to be shot at without result." After all, you probably are getting shot at, figuratively speaking. Having been through a number of turnaround situations (most of which turned out successfully), I can impart some definite rules of the road.

The first thing you should do is decide if the turnaround is possible. Sometimes you are faced with a situation where the handwriting is on the wall and despite your best efforts, success is not in the cards. It is better to discover this early so you do not have to spend your time and money on a losing cause.

For example, I was once hired to help turn around a struggling young company that had brilliant technology but poor marketing and sales results. It only took me a couple of weeks to determine that the fault was not in the specifics of the marketing and sales programs, but rather with the CEO. This guy was a dinosaur who was totally closed to any new ideas. He wanted to do things his way, and this was even more important to him than saving his company. You can probably guess the outcome – I resigned from the endeavor and watched from the sidelines as the company imploded.

So what do you need to make a turnaround happen? Here is the short list of necessary elements:

1. Willing and supportive executives (unlike the CEO mentioned above).

2. A budget necessary to sustain the turnaround effort.

3. The people resources necessary to sustain the turn-around effort.

4. A product or service that has an identified value proposition.

If you are a consultant or have been freshly hired to do the turnaround, you will face a different set of challenges than if you are an existing employee. You will have the advantage of the *outside aura*. It is amazing how often employees' opinions are ignored but some guy from the outside comes in and his words are treated as if they were written in stone on Mount Sinai.

Depending on the pathologies of the current situation, you may not have the luxury of a lot of thinking and planning time. You may need to act more like an emergency room doctor than a specialist, and get the patient stable before attempting the long-term cure. In this case, you will need to quickly assess the situation and make very fast decisions, based on factors like:

- Level of commitment from the board and senior management.

- Strength and loyalty of the existing sales and marketing staff.

- Capabilities and loyalty of the existing customer base.

- Major problems, both actual and perceived.

- Past and present budgets.

- Competitive landscape.

There are two very important things to remember in the early stages. First, people will be watching to see if you stumble early (with some perhaps hoping that you do). You should be careful not to make grandiose promises. Your early enthusiastic projections can come back to haunt you, so it is better to under-promise and over-deliver than vice versa. Second, ask for the resources you need early, while you are still in the honeymoon stage. This may sound counterintuitive, but if you deliver early success on a meager budget, they will often try to give you less, not more, going forward.

On a similar note, make sure you establish your authority (span of control) early. Any ground you give up early will be difficult to regain later. And do not make the mistake of thinking that everyone is your friend. I've seen many talented marketing executives scuttled by entrenched but unproductive sales VPs and vice versa. I hope that this will not happen to you, but it is better to hope for the best while preparing for the worst.

Do a quick but thorough assessment of the people you have to work with. Start with the internal staff. Where are the valuable skill sets? Which people are the keepers and which are hurting the organization? Which are truly motivated and which are just collecting paychecks?

Be careful here to understand the politics and alliances. Vendors can be of great help in a turnaround so make sure you get to know them. You can also cut costs by renegotiating vendor contracts. And by all means, listen to their ideas for improving results. Their perspectives can enhance and clarify what you are hearing from the inside.

You should also do a thorough review of customers. Despite the difficulties, there are probably certain customer segments that are profitable and others that are not worth the costs and trouble to maintain. The point is to focus like a laser on the profitable segments and ignore the others. You can go back and revisit underperforming segments later, but not early in the process.

Once you have completed your analysis of the overall situation, customers, and human elements, you need to dive into the numbers. Review the chapter on "How to Measure Your Marketing Success" for the specifics of what you should be quantifying. You need to quickly find out whether there are any aspects of marketing and sales that are working and can be leveraged and expanded. You can probably find some non-working or marginal programs to kill.

This is also the time to put on your *manufacturing* hat and analyze your marketing and sales assembly line to find the weaknesses. The chapter on "How to Build a Powerful Lead Engine" will help you do this. Chances are, you will find problems in one of five areas:

1. Not enough inquiries coming in to the top of the funnel. Address this by generating more inquiries.

2. Plenty of inbound inquiries but few are turning into qualified leads. Address this by instituting a good lead qualification process.

3. Leads are being qualified in good numbers, but few are showing up as opportunities in the sales pipeline. Ad-

dress this by examining what sales reps are doing with their qualified leads.

4. Plenty of opportunities but poor metrics when it comes to converting them to closed deals. Address this with a careful review and revamp of sales processes.

5. Inability to monitor the four preceding metrics. This is probably due to a lack of knowledge of how to measure the end-to-end process (that is why they hired you) or because you do not have the right CRM and marketing analytics technology. Address this by implementing the low-cost yet functional Fusion Marketing technologies mentioned in this book.

Go for the Low-Hanging Fruit

If you are faced with a really tough marketing and sales environment, it may be necessary to get some quick victories under your belt in order to buy time to carefully plan for the future. To use a sports analogy, you are like the new coach of a losing football team. They fired the old coach and you do not want to suffer the same fate. You have no illusions about getting your team to the Super Bowl this year. But what you really need is a few wins to take the fans' (and owner's) minds off last year's debacle while you rebuild the team.

Here are some areas where you may find early wins—otherwise known as low-hanging fruit:

- Existing Customer Base – Look for low-cost up-sell and cross-sell opportunities.

- Extending Contracts – Incentivize existing customers to increase the length of their contracts.

- Competitors – Borrow ideas that have worked/are working for competitors.

- Lower Cost of Acquisition – Replace higher cost media such as print advertising, direct mail and trade show exhibiting with lower cost media such as email and social media.

- Offers – Review the chapter on offers and test them until you find one or more that can boost your leads and sales.

- Sales Force Incentives – Selectively apply incentives to encourage greater results from the sales department.

- Partners – Explore ways to incentivize your channel or strategic partners to increase sales.

- Lead Revival Opportunities – Reconnect with all qualified leads from the past twelve to eighteen months. This is a low-cost and potentially lucrative source of new business.

Another area of low-hanging fruit to consider is products and pricing. Is the existing product structure working, or can it be changed to drive more revenue? Look at your cost of goods, margins, profitability, and lifetime value. You may find that you are under-pricing in relation to the rest of the marketplace, and if so, this is an excellent opportunity to gain additional revenue and profitability. Conversely, you may be over-pricing, and this could be costing you revenue. You can also look at ways to increase the value (and pricing) while adding little to the cost structure.

To Be or Not to Be (Honest)

Earlier in my career, I was VP of marketing for a well-known software company. After two weeks on the job, I was given some unpleasant facts of what had been going on. I asked my boss (the COO), "Why didn't you tell me about these issues during the hiring process?" He replied sheepishly, "Because you probably wouldn't have taken the job if I was honest with you." Actually, I would still have taken the job because I liked the industry and the turnaround was doable. However, I certainly watched the COO carefully from that point, and judged him on his actions instead of his words.

There are times when you should be careful about sharing all the facts with your team. I am not saying that you should lie; rather, you should be circumspect about what you share. However, unless you believe that sharing the whole truth will scare your good employees into leaving, or cause their productivity to plummet, it is usually better to be up-front about the challenges you face. This can create a true team atmosphere that will not only serve you well during the turnaround phase, but also post-turnaround.

Success Tip: Turnaround situations can be very tough but also offer great rewards.

Chapter 37

Produce Big Results with a Small Budget

"You can fool all of the people all of the time if the advertising is right and the budget is big enough."

– Joseph E. Levine

M any small-to medium-sized businesses fail due to a lack of an effective marketing and sales program. Entrepreneurs may be very good at their core business, but know very little about marketing. This is particularly true for companies where the founder may be a genius at designing complex products but lacks even a cursory knowledge of the marketing process. Certain people suffer from the theory espoused by Ralph Waldo Emerson, "If you build a better mousetrap, the world will beat a path to your door." They are innocently caught up in a love for their own products or services and believe the world will indeed beat a path to their door when prospects hear about the fantastic new product. This attitude is wrong, dangerous, and not in line with the practices of Fusion Marketing. In fact, more often than not, superior marketing beats a superior product. Of course, you are golden if you have both.

Another reason for failure is that an effective marketing campaign is disciplined, hard work. Since marketing is probably not what motivated the entrepreneur to open his or her business, it receives less priority than product development and other tasks. Marketing also often comes up short when scarce funds are allocated. Sadly, there are start-up companies that spend tens of thousands of dollars on extravagant furniture and equipment, while complaining that there is nothing left for marketing.

New companies also make a mistake by hiring expensive advertising agencies that are incapable of cost-effective, low-budget marketing. Or they hire marketing and sales talent from big companies, and these people are often clueless about how to get results on a limited budget. So if you are in a small company, be careful about hiring the hotshot from a big company to come solve your problems. It often doesn't work. This is not to say that everyone from a big company is incapable of being effective with a smaller budget—some are great no matter the company size.

Small to medium businesses and start-ups face two major obstacles not shared by larger, entrenched companies. First, if you happen to be a small fish in a large pond, you will be confronted by competitors with much larger advertising and marketing budgets. Second, you may have to spend a larger percentage of your revenues on marketing than older, established organizations.

Given the reality of this situation, you need to squeeze as much efficiency as possible out of every dollar. Be assured that you can do a lot on a limited budget, and expensive does not always mean better. I've often used limited-budget strategies to beat the big players and you can do the same. And the lessons you learn by doing it the frugal way will serve you well, no matter how successful you become, or how far your marketing budget expands. Here are a collection of small budget strategies and tactics you can use to beat the big guys:

Small Budget Website Strategies

1. Do not overbuild your Website. There are ways to create an impressive site using less-complex open source or template approaches.

2. If possible, have an easy-to-remember Website address that relates to what your company does.

3. List your Web address (URL) on all of your corporate materials.

4. Make sure your Website is optimized for organic search terms. This is a low-cost strategy that will make you much easier to find.

5. Try narrowly focused low-cost pay per click search terms.

6. Give some information away for free to increase your Website stickiness.

7. Create many links with other sites to increase your search engine visibility.

8. Refresh your content often. Do not let the site go stale.

Small Budget Social Media Strategies

1. Start your own blog and comment on other blogs.

2. Always list your Web address on your blog postings and any electronic communication.

3. Leverage LinkedIn and other networking sites.

4. Use Twitter to find relevant posts and prospects.

5. Be controversial (but not too controversial) to attract attention.

6. Choose a niche where you can be an expert.

7. Write articles and get them published in online media.

8. Focus on one or two social media outlets. This concentrated attention will bring more attention than throwing your efforts at five or six outlets.

Small Budget Email Strategies

1. Work hard to build your email prospect file of opt-in names. This will be a gold mine of low-cost leads and sales.

2. Include a promotional message and your Website address as part of your standard email signature.

3. Provide links to valuable information in your emails, not just product pitches.

4. Make your emails interesting and/or unusual.

5. Run your email copy through a spam detection tool like EmailExam (emailexam.com), Acxiom Digital (acxiomdigital.com), or Lyris ContentChecker (lyris.com) to ensure your emails will not be caught in the spam filters.

6. Have an easy opt-out process. You do not want to keep sending emails to people who want to be removed from your list.

Small Budget Print Ad Strategies

1. Always include a coupon in your ads. Tear-out coupons can boost print ad response by twenty percent.

2. Offer both a telephone and a Web form. If possible,

use a toll-free phone number. The combination of a Web form and a toll-free number can increase results up to thirty-five percent.

3. Always include a strong call to action.

4. Instead of large ads, consider running smaller ads more frequently.

5. Do not give up on a productive ad too soon. Let it run longer, build recognition with frequency, and save the cost of creating a new advertisement.

6. Test type-only ads. They are less expensive to produce, and sometimes pull better than ads with graphics.

7. Negotiate with publications. They are often flexible with new advertisers since they want your future business. For monthly publications, try to negotiate the "twelve times" rate, even if you are only committing to two or three issues. This can result in a considerable savings.

8. Consider running in regional editions of national publications. This can give you the stature of the national advertiser at far less cost.

9. Become a standby advertiser. If the publication has space that opens up at the last minute, it will often sell it to you for one-third to one-half the published rate.

10. Check with a publication's advertisers. However, don't just call those that are currently advertising. Also call the companies that ran ads six to twelve months before. You can save a lot of trouble and expense by making a few phone calls.

Small Budget Direct Marketing Strategies

1. Target your lists more effectively by using demographics, psychographics, and some of the other list segmenting tools available. The object is to mail fewer packages and achieve greater response.

2. Test your mailing and telemarketing in small quantities before committing large sums to full-blown programs. Equally important, use the information you learn on every program to make the next work better.

3. Try a postcard mailer. The production costs are low, the first-class postage is less expensive than letter mail, and they pull very well. You can drive prospects to a Web form or toll-free telephone number.

4. Cut back on four-color process direct mail packages. Unless you sell food, magazines, resort properties, or other products requiring excellent graphic reproduction, you can probably pull as much response using two-color printing.

5. Consider mailing with third-class postage instead of first-class. Depending on whether you presort the file, this will save you a great amount of money, and most prospects will not notice the difference. The exception is with time-sensitive offers, since third-class mail can take a week longer to arrive than first-class.

6. If you mail to large numbers on a national basis, or send highly concentrated mailings into local or regional areas, use postal pre-sorting to lower postage costs.

Other Cost-Cutting Ideas

1. If you are a small company (a flea), find a big company (a dog) to partner with. This will make it much easier for you to sell to bigger companies.

2. Read the chapter on public relations carefully and begin carrying out its advice. PR is a low-effort, high-reward vehicle that is often under-utilized by small-budget marketers.

3. Be persistent. Remember the *eight times* rule: You don't have to spend a lot of money on each communication, but you must repeat your message up to eight times to gain prospect awareness.

4. Write handwritten personal notes to prospects and customers. They are cheap but make a big impact.

5. Ask for referrals. They are much easier to sell, at lower cost.

6. Utilize experts. An expert's advice will cost you something in the short term, but can save you money and aggravation in the long term.

7. List your primary products and services on your stationery and business card, or anything else you give to potential buyers.

8. Since consistency is vital for those with small budgets, make sure every one of your marketing efforts supports and reinforces your unique selling proposition (USP).

9. Sharpen your bargaining skills. Media outlets are hungry for business and many have unsold inventory. Use this to your advantage by negotiating aggressively.

One other important principle to practice is leverage. Try to create content once and use it in multiple marketing scenarios. This is less expensive and time-consuming, and the consistency of message is important.

Success Tip: You do not need a large budget to make a big impact. But you do need to be a smart and aggressive marketer.

Chapter 38

Summary – Final Thoughts for Fusion Marketing Success

"An invasion of armies can be resisted, but not an idea whose time has come."

– Victor Hugo

I have thrown a lot of content at you in this book, including core principles, prospect identification, creative strategy, media tactics, market planning, and building a great team. Most important, I have shared the techniques that allow you to create an unstoppable marketing and sales machine. I hope that you have already implemented some of these strategies and are preparing to implement others. To end our journey together, I would like to leave you with ten important reminders from the book. Regardless of what else you do, if you follow these fundamentals, you will achieve greater success.

1. To create a steady growth in revenue, you must have an identified and replicable framework, which becomes a model for consistency and sustainable success. This framework is the essence of the marketing and sales machine.

2. You must thoroughly understand your competitors

and customers to be successful — especially your customers. Knowledge, as well as the ability to quickly deploy that knowledge, is the fuel that powers the marketing and sales machine.

3. You can achieve great marketplace awareness with a message that is compelling and consistent, and most important, the message must be highly relevant to those who are in a position to buy what you are selling.

4. Focus all the resources (dollars, people, and technology) in your organization toward common goals, and eliminate resources that are not directed at these goals.

5. Establish metrics that are quantifiable, motivating, and achievable. These metrics must become a driving force in your organization because they always tell you how well the marketing and sales machine is running.

6. Utilize technology and system resources tactically to support strategic business processes. Technology is a great asset, but only if it supports your business processes.

7. You must monitor and improve every part of the end-to-end marketing and sales process framework—there are NO unimportant steps. Strength in each part of the process will give you exponential results.

8. Sales must define exactly what a qualified lead is—then allow marketing to do its job in delivering that lead. You must have agreement between these two organizations in order to convert more leads into customers.

9. If there are any gaps or disagreements between the

goals and deliverables of the marketing and sales organizations, you must eliminate these gaps. Consistency and unity are more important to the organization than a search for lofty but non-integrated goals from specific departments.

10. No matter where you are today, you can begin right now and make constant improvement in your marketing and sales operations. It is usually not a stroke of brilliance that will get you to your goal, but rather, a series of smaller actions that together have large impact.

Finally, you always have the choice of whether to act, or sit on your hands waiting for the right circumstances. Sometimes, the right circumstances refuse to appear so you need to take action despite the lack of clarity. I leave you with a great quote that appears in *The 6 Imperatives of Marketing* by Allan J. Magrath.

> *"Every morning in Africa, a gazelle wakes up. It knows it must run faster than the fastest lion or it will be killed.*
>
> *Every morning a lion wakes up. It knows it must outrun the slowest gazelle or it will starve to death. It doesn't matter if you're a lion or a gazelle; when the sun comes up you'd better be running."*
>
> *–Unknown*

My last bit of advice to you is to start running.
Much success and happiness,

Christopher Ryan
cryan@fusionmarketingpartners.com
www.fusionmarketingpartners.com

About the Author

Christopher Ryan is the managing director of Fusion Marketing Partners. Chris has twenty-five years of marketing, technology, and senior management experience, and is a widely known expert in business-to-business marketing, sales strategy, systems, and processes. As both a services provider and in-house marketing executive, Chris has played a transformative role in driving marketing and sales programs that achieve the desired results and create alignment and synergy between the sales and marketing operations.

Prior to founding Fusion Marketing Partners, Chris Ryan served as Vice President of Marketing at SpringCM, the world's leading provider of on-demand content management solutions. Before that, Chris was Vice President of Marketing at Stellent, Inc., a $125 million supplier of enterprise content management (ECM) software and services, as well as Vice President of Worldwide Product Marketing for FrontRange Solutions, Inc., a $100 million supplier of customer relationship management (CRM) software. Chris was also co-founder and Chief Marketing Officer of Saligent Software, Inc., a marketing automation software and services company. Earlier, Chris held senior management positions at noted technology firms PeopleSoft, Sybase, and Group 1 Software.

Chris is known as an outstanding communicator and has presented keynote addresses and breakout sessions at numerous conferences on marketing and technology. For three years, *Target Marketing* magazine named Chris as one of the Top 100 U.S. Marketers. Chris has written three other books on marketing and information technology and has been an instructor and lecturer at the College of Notre Dame, University of Colorado, and Montgomery College.

About Fusion Marketing Partners

Fusion Marketing Partners diagnoses and adds value to every part of your marketing-through-sales processes, with the objective of helping you generate more sales revenue from every dollar you invest in people and programs. We call this *Creating an Unstoppable Marketing and Sales Machine* because you will have a framework for generating awareness, qualified leads, and revenue that is repeatable and predictable.

As illustrated in the graphic below, we achieve great benefits for our clients by synchronizing and optimizing all the elements of their marketing and sales strategies including programs, content, people, processes, budget, and technology. The FMP team has expertise in constructing a value proposition for you that is compelling—and then delivering this message to the right target prospect at the right time, using the most appropriate media tools. Most important, we make sure that you have streamlined processes and effective underlying technologies to drive success.

The Fusion Marketing Process for Creating Unstoppable Marketing and Sales Machines

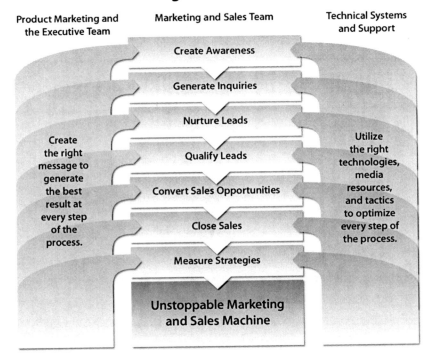

Benefits to You

By following the proven strategies of Fusion Marketing Partners:

- You will know exactly which parts of the marketing and sales process are working and those that are not working.

- You will discover the right model for maximizing revenue-generation.

- You will know the specific steps necessary to improve every part of the marketing- through-sales process.

- You will have actionable metrics that help you quickly get on track and keep you there.

- You will understand the strengths of your existing marketing and sales processes and personnel and know how to best utilize these resources to achieve the desired results.

If you would like to explore how a relationship with Fusion Marketing Partners can assist you, please send us a note at info@fusionmarketing-partners.com.

Index

Breinigsville, PA USA
14 October 2009
225782BV00003B/1/P

9 780982 539729